Legal Research and Writing Skills in Ireland

LEGAL RESEARCH AND WRITING SKILLS IN IRELAND

By

Dr EDANA RICHARDSON

and

Dr OLLIE BARTLETT

CLARUS PRESS

Published by
Clarus Press Ltd,
Griffith Campus,
South Circular Road,
Dublin 8.
www.claruspress.ie

Typeset by
Gough Typesetting Services,
Dublin

Printed by
SprintPrint
Dublin

ISBN
978-1-911611-48-6

A catalogue record for this book is available from the British Library

Disclaimer
Whilst every effort has been made to ensure that the contents of this book are
accurate, neither the publisher and/or author(s) can accept responsibility for
any errors or omissions or loss occasioned to any person acting or refraining
from acting as result of any material in this publication.

Preface

Few people choose to study law at third level specifically to learn about legal research and writing. However, being a skilled legal researcher and writer will stand to you not just throughout your degree, but into your professional life. As a law student, a solicitor or a barrister (or, indeed, in many other careers) you will be expected to research and write effectively.

Yet people often ignore the research and writing portion of studying or practising law. Instead, they focus on the substantive legal issues. While such substantive legal issues are, of course, important, if you do not dedicate time and energy towards strengthening your legal research and writing skills, your analysis of the law risks being incomplete or even incomprehensible.

Legal Research and Writing Skills in Ireland offers a practical and accessible guide for aspiring and current law students, as well as legal practitioners in the early stages of their career. Structured across three parts, this book takes you from initial research planning through to proofreading the final version of your written product. It also provides guidance on specific situations in which legal research and writing will be relevant, such as emails, written assignments and letters. Worked examples and practical tips are used throughout the book to reinforce your understanding. Where helpful, templates and checklists have been included to provide you with a starting point in your own legal research and writing.

The advice and tips included in this book are based on our experience in legal practice and academia.

We would like to thank Joseph Harrington for his helpful comments on a draft of this book and Brónagh Heverin for her guidance on various chapters. We would also like to thank David McCartney of Clarus Press for approaching us to write this book and his continued guidance throughout and Shane Gough of Gough Typesetting Services for making the finished book look so polished.

Edana Richardson
Ollie Bartlett
March 2021

Table of Contents

PART II
THE WRITING PROCESS

Table of Cases

Table of Legislation

Chapter 1

An Introduction to Legal Research and Writing

1.1 Aims of the book

Being a good law student or a good lawyer is about more than knowing the law. It is important that you are able to find, analyse and articulate that law – research and writing are, therefore, core legal skills that you should strive to develop during, and well beyond, your law degree.

Legal Research and Writing Skills in Ireland aims to be a practical guide to legal research and writing. It provides you with detailed guidance on how to plan and structure your research, how to write effectively and how to support what you write with authority. It also gives you practical tips on how to be a better legal researcher and writer and step-by-step guides on the key stages of legal research and writing. The book will use illustrative examples that are all based on the same fictional scenario (set out in Section 1.5 below) to demonstrate how the points made in each chapter can be put into practice. While the skills discussed in this book are applicable to anyone undertaking a piece of legal research or writing, *Legal Research and Writing Skills in Ireland* will be of particular relevance to law students and junior practitioners in Ireland.

What this book does not cover is legal drafting in the sense of creating legal documents, such as contracts, court orders, deeds or legislation. This is a specific skill that you will learn should you go into practice as a solicitor or barrister and requires you to consider the legal implications of what you write. Instead, this book seeks to provide you with skills to help you to research and write clearly and elegantly in a variety of situations, such as emails, presentation slides and essays. This is not, however, to say that legal writing is not important when it comes to drafting legal documents – all drafting involves legal writing; not all legal writing takes the form of drafting. Documents that you draft should, therefore, still follow the rules set out in this book.

1.2 Overview of this book

Legal Research and Writing Skills in Ireland is organised in three parts. The first part (Chapters 2 and 3) focuses on the research process. The second part (Chapters 4, 5 and 6) focuses on the writing process. The third part (Chapter 7) focuses on how to use your research and writing skills in situations that you will encounter during and after your degree. This book, therefore, follows the process of undertaking a piece of legal research and writing from start to finish. As such, its chapters can be read sequentially in order to build your understanding of these core legal skills. However, the individual chapters of *Legal Research and Writing Skills in Ireland* can also be referenced individually when specific guidance is needed. Chapter 7, in particular, is structured to allow you to refer to the specific type of document that you are preparing.

The contents of each chapter are outlined in more detail below.

- **Chapter 2** discusses research planning. This chapter will take you through a process of research planning that can be followed for any piece of legal writing that you are asked to complete – not only during your degree, but also during the first years of your career.
- **Chapter 3** outlines how to search for sources of legal information. A vast amount of legal information exists today, the majority of it accessible through digital means. You may feel overwhelmed by the amount of information that is available to you or be unsure of where to look for information and what you should do when the information you want does not immediately materialise. This chapter will help you to understand the sources of information that you are likely to engage with and to navigate the various databases and search engines that you can use to locate the information that you need.
- **Chapter 4** discusses the foundational elements of good writing. It goes back to basics and looks at spelling, grammar and punctuation, how to use capital letters, defined terms and acronyms and the presentation of quotations. These are aspects of writing that you should

not be getting wrong, not least in a legal context where a misspelled word or a misplaced comma could change the meaning of a sentence.

- **Chapter 5** builds on the basics identified in Chapter 4 and considers how legal writing can be made more effective. In doing so, this chapter emphasises the importance of clear, succinct and accurate written work, the need to be mindful of presentation and optics in your legal writing, and the importance of proofreading.

- **Chapter 6** looks specifically at referencing your work using footnotes. It considers the reasons why we footnote and provides tips on how to cite various sources that might be relevant in your legal writing.

- **Chapter 7** discusses how the advice provided in the preceding six chapters on effective research and writing could be used in certain specific situations that you will commonly encounter during and after your degree. This final chapter, therefore, discusses, and provides tips on, how to plan and write a dissertation proposal, a written assignment, emails, letters and the written portion of a presentation.

1.3 The importance of learning legal skills

From the first day of your law degree, you should start thinking of yourself as a legal researcher and writer. Whether you are writing a 2,000 word undergraduate essay, a 20,000 word postgraduate dissertation, an 80,000 word academic book, a two (or 20) page memo for the partner in your team, or written submissions for an upcoming court hearing, you will need to be a skilled researcher and writer if you want to produce an excellent piece of legal work. The sooner you believe that you are a legal researcher and writer, rather than just a passive recipient of knowledge, the sooner you will start producing great legal work.

Good research and writing skills are essential if you wish to successfully enter the legal (or many other) professions. Besides helping you to become a better law student, the main objective of teaching you legal skills during law school is to ensure that by the time you wish to enter a professional environment, you will have the necessary research and writing competences already in place. In legal practice, virtually everything that you do will be supported by strong research and writing skills. Writing clear advice letters, conducting effective client interviews, negotiating a contractual provision, making persuasive arguments in court, drafting accurate legal documents, and other legal practice activities all require you to be a practically skilled lawyer, as well as a knowledgeable one.

Law firms want solicitors (and trainee solicitors) who have the necessary skills in place. Few law firms have time to extensively train their trainee solicitors in the basics of doing legal research, the rules of grammar or how to use capital letters, so they will expect their new recruits to already be able to find, read, cite and write about the law effectively. Law firms need their solicitors to make the most of the time that clients are paying for – no client, and therefore no law firm, will be happy with paying for 20 hours of work if that work could have been produced in ten (or fewer) hours. Law firms want solicitors who will produce high quality and efficient work, and to help you to achieve both of these traits, you need to be a competent researcher and writer. Finally, it is a matter of professional integrity that solicitors gain sufficient basic skills to be capable of providing accurate and competent advice to clients. Law firms do not want solicitors who may do harm to a client's interests because they are prone to making mistakes in their research or writing.

Even outside of the legal profession, the research and writing competences that you should aim to develop during and beyond your law degree will serve you well in any profession. These skills are transferrable to virtually every professional role. Any professional will need to understand the range of information they have to work with, know how to access the information needed to achieve their work goals, read efficiently, and write clearly and effectively. As a result, committing to learning and developing your legal skills will put you in an advantageous position for entering the professional world, whatever profession you pursue.

To help you to build competence in legal skills, many law departments now require that you take a module in legal skills early in your degree (and some even offer advanced legal skills modules in later years). The purpose of teaching such a module early in your degree is to help you to immediately start building the legal skills that you will be asked to use in each of your substantive law modules. A separate legal skills module provides you with the opportunity to learn and practise legal skills. It is a space that is dedicated to identifying and exploring legal skills, so that you can more clearly see and understand the nature of the skills that your lecturers are asking you to demonstrate (and on which they are assessing you). If you have a space to specifically focus on learning about and developing legal skills, you will do so more quickly and confidently. If you build competence in legal skills early on, you will be able to progress with your substantive legal learning more quickly and confidently – having better legal skills enables you to more readily understand and analyse the substantive law you are taught.

However, having the dedicated space and training on legal skills is only half the story. For the objectives above to be realised, further input is required – this further input consists of you giving attention to the learning of legal skills and being dedicated in your practice of these skills after you leave third-level education. You will only improve your legal skills if you put conscious effort into thinking about them and practising them. Hoping that your legal skills will improve as you do more essays or as you become a trainee solicitor is not enough. Nor is it enough to assume that your legal skills will improve simply though exposure to a legal skills course. Building your legal skills must happen in the same way as you would build any other practical skill – it must be done gradually and methodically, and it must be founded on practice and feedback. Becoming a competent, and in time excellent, researcher and writer takes time, practice and thought.

1.4 How to learn legal skills

The previous section explained the importance of treating the learning and practice of legal skills seriously – this section now considers how you should do this. The core legal skills addressed in this book are:

- rigorous planning of your work;
- efficient and effective searching for, and reading of, sources of legal information;
- clear and impactful writing; and
- accurate citation of legal sources.

The graphic below represents the essential elements of how to learn about and practise these legal skills.

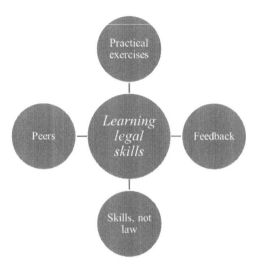

1.4.1 Practical exercises

The first element of learning legal skills—practising and repetition—has already been hinted at above. The best way to build competence in legal skills is by practising them. As is the case with your substantive law modules, reading academic literature is an important part of learning legal skills. This much might appear obvious – doing so will enable you to deepen your understanding of the theories that explain why building competence in legal skills is essential. However, another similarity between your substantive modules and your legal skills module is that the completion of practical work is an important part of learning legal skills. In the same way that you would write practice essays, engage in tutorials, or complete quizzes and worksheets for your substantive law modules, to build competence in legal skills you must also devote time to practical exercises designed to help you to refine these skills. These may be provided to you as part of your legal skills module. Alternatively, sample exercises designed to help you build legal skills can be found easily online. Try to complete these practice exercises on a regular basis. You will find that by regularly spending a small amount of time thinking specifically about your legal skills and putting these skills into practice, you will build competence in them much faster, compared to if you only paid attention to them when writing an essay or revising for an exam.

1.4.2 Feedback

Although your substantive law modules may not devote much (or any) time to specifically talking about legal skills, your lecturers may still be able to provide you with feedback on how you are using your legal skills in their modules. This will take the form of feedback provided on your assignments. When writing up feedback on an essay or problem question, lecturers will often comment on the level of skill with which it was produced, as well as the level of legal knowledge displayed. You may receive comments on how well you answered the question, how good your level of analysis was, how clear your writing was, whether you structured your writing well, whether you cited your sources accurately, or whether you demonstrated enough evidence of independent reading. You should pay close attention to these comments whenever you receive them – they will identify the legal skills that you need to practise more often, and (depending on the level of detail in the comments) what you should try to focus on doing next time you undertake a piece of legal writing.

If you are unsure of the meaning of any feedback that you get, make an appointment to discuss that feedback with your lecturer. Practising your legal skills is essential, but a few minutes spent discussing a particularly difficult skill element with your lecturer can be more helpful for your understanding of that skill than several hours spent practising alone.

1.4.3 Skills, not law

Whenever you practise, or look at feedback that you have received on, a piece of legal writing, you should do so with the following in mind – you are trying to improve your legal skills, not just your knowledge of the law. It is easy to assume that a legal skills module is just another vehicle for teaching you about the law, albeit in a more practical manner. However, the effective development of legal skills requires students to discard these ideas and remind themselves that their work on legal skills is exactly that – work on *skills*, not law.

A law degree serves a far broader purpose than just delivering knowledge about the law. Law degrees must also teach you how to think, research, and write in a 'lawyerly' manner. Once you get into the habit of thinking about your legal studies in this way, you will be able to build your legal skills more efficiently when you sit down to practise your legal research and writing or when you read feedback on your legal writing. When you do this, your focus should be on the learning of skills, rather than the learning of law – concentrate on understanding and applying the practical techniques that you are practising.

1.4.4 Peers

Your peers will be an essential resource for you during your degree and once you enter a professional environment. Talking to your peers about legal skills is the final key element of effective legal skills learning. As a law student, much of your time will be spent finding, reading, writing about, and citing the law. You and your peers will, therefore, have far more to talk about with respect to applying your legal skills than the actual content of the law. Moreover, it is a near certainty that if you are struggling with an aspect of research or writing, one of your friends will be (or will have been) experiencing similar problems. Therefore, talk to your peers about legal skills. Compare how you have been doing things, share the issues that you have been having, discuss the solutions that you have trying out. Your peers may be able to give you ideas or suggestions that you would never have thought of alone. You could be pointed in the direction of useful resources or additional exercises that you did not know existed. Remember that you spend your degree time not just with your law lecturers, but also with your law peers – those peers are a valuable resource.

1.5 Fictional scenario

Set out below is a fictional scenario. This scenario will form the basis of all illustrative examples used throughout this book.

> The local youth mixed basketball team (the 'Cispheil Nets') is coached by Emily Holloway, a one-time Olympic basketball player who left the United States' national basketball team in disgrace after head-butting an opposing team's mascot during a particularly tense warm-up session.
>
> One Monday in September last year, Emily, together with members of the Cispheil Nets, attended a friendly tournament at a local sports complex. The team did very well, and they were in good spirits. Following the tournament, Emily asked the children to return to their bus (which was parked outside) quickly and quietly. Most of them did just that. However, just as they were about to exit the sports complex, 9-year-old Caden Goldsmith's nose started to bleed, and he burst into tears.

Caden is the youngest member of the Cispheil Nets. Caden also has haemophilia (meaning that it takes longer for his blood to clot) and Emily had been given training on how to react in such circumstances. Knowing that she had to act quickly, Emily held Caden's head back as they rushed to the bathroom. There, Emily tried to stop the bleeding. After a few minutes, the bleeding stopped although Caden was still very upset. Happy that Caden was physically alright, Emily slowly led him towards the exit of the sports complex.

As Emily and Caden neared the exit they heard a commotion. Emily turned around to see what was happening. Two men were standing by the cash register at the sports complex's shop; one held a knife above his head and the other held what looked like a hand grenade in his right hand. The man with the hand grenade held it up and calmly said, 'I do not want to hurt anyone, but if anyone moves, I will do it'.

Hiding behind a display of tennis rackets, Emily and Caden were hidden from the armed men. Nevertheless, Emily decided to risk running for the exit. She grabbed Caden's hand and pulled him into a standing position. They ran towards the exit. In the confusion, Caden accidentally kicked a tennis racket, which sent the whole display crashing to the ground. This startled the man with the hand grenade causing him to spin around and hurl the hand grenade in the direction of Emily and Caden. The hand grenade missed them but hit a nearby display of glass trophies sending shards of broken glass flying. While Emily and Caden managed to avoid most of the destruction, a piece of broken glass hit Caden in the arm. This caused a cut and Caden fell forward. Emily picked him up and continued running for the exit – they both got out without further injury. Due to Caden's haemophilia, the cut on his arm was bleeding profusely. Emily did all that she could to stop the bleeding until the ambulance arrived and took Caden to hospital. Caden lost a lot of blood and suffered brain damage as a result.

Emily is distraught at what happened.

Part I

The Research Process

Planning Your Research

2.1 Learning why good research is good research

Good legal writing starts with good legal research. Yet, beginning the research for a piece of legal writing is often the hardest part of the entire process. Students ask how and where they are supposed to 'start' their essay, and much essay feedback relates in some way to what students did or did not do in the earliest stages of a piece of legal writing – that is, what they did or did not do when planning their research.

Research planning can be undertaken in a logical, step-by-step manner that will reliably provide the foundation for a relevant and clear piece of legal writing. As well as considering how to conduct legal research, you should also invest time in thinking more broadly about *why* legal research is important and the broader practical and cognitive underpinnings of good legal research. Learning how to conduct legal research should be about learning why good research is good research.[1]

This chapter proposes approaches to conducting good legal research. It is not, however, exhaustive and you may develop your own approach to legal research that you find works for you. Try to understand why the approaches discussed in this chapter contribute to good legal research and use them as a means of discovering further, more complex insights about legal research for yourself. The explanations, examples and practical tips given in this chapter are designed to help you do this.

---

[1] Paul D Callister, 'Thinking like a Research Expert: Schemata for Teaching Complex Problem-Solving Skills' (2009) 28 Legal References Services Quarterly 31, 31–32.

> **Practical Tip**
>
> This chapter is aimed primarily at third-level students writing essays and dissertations. However, its advice for identifying the purpose of a piece of legal writing and planning your research will be relevant to other pieces of legal writing, such as case notes, mooting submissions and letters of advice to clients.

Beginning your research consists of two main phases: (1) identifying your research question(s); and (2) planning your approach to your research question(s).

2.2 Identifying the research question(s)

2.2.1 What is a research question, and why do you need one?

One of the most frequently received pieces of feedback for a law student is that his or her piece of legal writing has 'not answered the question'. Law students might think some of the following in response to this feedback.

- What does it mean to 'answer the question'?
- What if the assignment brief did not give me a clear question?
- What parts of the question are the most important?
- How much am I expected to say?
- How do I know when I am done?

When a lecturer's feedback is that you have not answered the question, that lecturer is indicating that you need to improve the way in which you identify and respond to the research question that lies at the heart of the assignment. Every piece of legal research— from first year undergraduate essays to academic journal articles to letters of legal advice—starts with one or more research questions. Identifying the right research question(s) to guide the piece of legal writing that you are about to undertake is a key legal skill. It is just as important as being able to read and analyse the law – probably even more so. Without identifying the right research question(s) to guide your work, you are more likely to provide analysis that does not satisfactorily address the legal issues at stake.

A 'research question' could be defined as a summary of the core legal issue or problem that you want to resolve. It is usually a single sentence that poses a specific and focused question that is possible to answer in the space and time you have available. Others have defined a research question similarly, for example, as 'the initial identification of the legal issue or issues to be researched ... a preliminary statement of the problem'.[2]

Why is a research question so crucial to the success of your legal writing? There are several reasons.[3]

- An effective research question will define the boundaries of your research, so that you are not wasting time doing irrelevant reading.
- An effective research question will focus your research, so that you are doing the work that your lecturers want you to do. You might wonder why lecturers do not simply tell you what they want. The reason is that when you practise as a lawyer, clients will expect you as the legal professional to tell them what their legal problems and solutions are. They will not be able to tell you how to handle their legal issues – they are paying you to work that out for them.
- An effective research question enables you to structure your work clearly, so that you are addressing the legal issues in a way that the reader can follow and understand. You may need more than one research question if your assignment raises a sufficiently large number of distinct legal issues. A long and complicated research question is more likely to lead you towards a convoluted structure, thus defeating the purpose of creating research questions in the first place. Constructing several short and clear research questions when appropriate will enable you to work out a clear and effective order in which to discuss the issues that you have identified.

Sometimes, the research question will be obvious from the assignment brief – you might simply be given a direct and well-defined question to answer.

---

[2] Caroline Osborne, 'The Legal Research Plan and the Research Log: An Examination of the Role of the Research Plan and Research Log in the Research Process' (2016) 35(3) Legal Reference Services Quarterly 179, 182.

[3] For an in-depth examination of the construction of research questions, and why constructing good research questions is important, see: Patrick White, *Developing Research Questions* (2nd edn, Palgrave 2017).

> **Example:**
>
> Assume that rather than the scenario set out in Chapter 1 of this book, you are undertaking a tort law assignment that simply consists of the following question:
>
> > *'Have the Irish courts created clear rules in relation to the imposition of duties of care on defendants who are being sued in negligence?'*
>
> In this situation, the assignment brief has already given you a clear research question to answer – this will make it easier for you to plan your research.

However, at other times your assignment brief will give you a quotation or statement, which you are instructed to 'discuss', perhaps 'with reference to' case law, statues or literature. You will also be given problem questions in which you are given a set of facts and then instructed to 'advise' a client on his, her or its legal position.

These types of assignment—particularly problem questions—are designed to reflect the realities of legal practice. Clients will come to you with either a discrete problem or a longer story, which may be quite fragmented or disjointed. That client will expect you to translate the information provided into a clear and logical set of legal issues, to which you will present the best legal solutions and advice.

In situations in which your assignment brief does not give you a direct research question, you will have to identify the important legal issues from the statements or facts with which you are presented. You will then need to create research question(s) so that you can begin investigating these issues. This is all part of the teaching and assessment purpose of the assignment – your lecturers are not only trying to give you knowledge about the law, but also trying to help you become more skilled in working out what core legal issues are at stake in a given situation.

> **Example:**
>
> Assume that your assignment is not a straightforward question, but instead looks something like this:
>
> > 'The Irish courts have routinely refused to endorse a subjective standard of care in negligence cases.
> >
> > Critically discuss this statement.'
>
> In this situation, the assignment brief has raised a legal issue, but has not provided a clear research question. Your first task must, therefore, be to create a research question from the statement that you are given.

2.2.2 How do you create a research question?

There are three basic steps to creating a useful research question.

(1)   **Identify the core legal issues raised by the assignment brief.**
   - Think about the brief carefully – what are the consequences or implications of the facts raised by the brief?
   - Think about the problems or unknowns that are created by those consequences or implications,[4] about which the law might have something to say.
   - Which of these problems or unknowns are the most pressing or salient? These will be the core legal issues raised by the assignment brief.

(2)   **Identify the research questions that you need.**
   - Think about how many core legal issues you have identified. For some assignments, especially problem questions, you may have identified several core legal issues.
   - Are any of the legal issues that you have identified closely related to each other? If so, you could group these together, and write one research question that deals with all of them.
   - Summarise each legal issue, or each distinct group of

---

4   Sometimes your lecturers will want you to demonstrate that you can identify, and then analyse, the obvious or common legal problems that arise in a particular situation. At other times, your lecturer will give you an open-ended assignment, which gives you the opportunity to identify and analyse what you subjectively perceive to be the main legal problems. Try to examine the brief and work out which type of assignment you are faced with. Terry Hutchinson and Nigel Duncan, 'Defining and describing what we do: Doctrinal legal research' (2012) 17(1) Deakin Law Review 83, 107.

legal issues, as a question. These will be your research questions.

(3)   Identify the essential 'parts' of each research question.
- Think about the individual points that you will need to discuss in order to answer each research question in a clear and satisfactory way.
- Decide what legal knowledge you will need in order to do this. Determine what outcomes you will need to demonstrate and what evidence you will need to provide.
- Set out these smaller points clearly and succinctly, in an order that is logical. This will help you to plan your answers to each research question.

You should ensure that you create your research question(s) in a way that also reflects any specific instructions or information that you have been given in the assignment brief. For example, if you have been asked to critically discuss a statement, you should ensure that your research question(s) will facilitate critical discussion. 'Do the Irish courts always refuse to endorse a subjective standard of care in negligence cases, and is there any evidence of them ever endorsing such a standard?' is a research question that will facilitate critical discussion. 'What do the Irish courts say about subjective standards of care in negligence cases?' is a research question that will facilitate a largely uncritical description of the law. The research question(s) that you create must also not overcomplicate the assignment brief. A research question that raises more issues and is far longer and more complex than the brief you have been given will not help you to focus or organise your work.

Write out your research question(s) and their essential parts somewhere – either on the assignment brief, at the top of your essay draft, in your notes or wherever is most convenient. By doing this, you ensure that you do not forget the core questions that are guiding your research.

Only once you have identified and made a note of your research question(s) will you be ready to start planning the research itself.

Example:

Let us look at the scenario set out in Chapter 1 of this book. What are the research questions that you need to create? Since this is a long fact pattern, you will likely need more than one research question to be able to provide a good response.

The first step of the process outlined above is to work out the core legal issues. When doing this in the context of a fact pattern, you will have to look carefully at the facts which you have been presented with – work out which facts are relevant to identifying the core legal issues, and which are irrelevant. You then need to think about the most pressing legal issues or legal unknowns. The following is a summary of how you could do this.

- The key facts are as follows: the first key fact is that Emily is aware of Caden's haemophilia. The second key fact is that two men enter the sports complex and appear to commence an armed robbery, with one man making clear that he will detonate what appears to be a hand grenade if anyone in the area moves. The third key fact is that the man with the grenade made his threat calmly and Emily and Caden are hidden from the armed men, yet Emily decides to make a run for the exit with Caden. The fourth key fact is that Caden accidentally knocks over the display of tennis rackets, causing a noise that leads to the man with the grenade throwing it. The fifth key fact is that, although the grenade misses Emily and Caden, the destruction it causes results in Caden being injured by flying glass shards. The sixth and final key fact is that due to Caden's haemophilia, and despite Emily's efforts, the amount of blood he loses as a result of his injury causes him to suffer brain damage.
- If you look at these facts, two main legal issues emerge. The first obvious issue is whether Emily has a duty to ensure that injury does not occur to Caden in this situation. Emily was clearly in a situation that could have turned violent. She also knew about Caden's haemophilia, which could drastically exacerbate even minor injuries. Is Emily legally responsible for ensuring that Caden does not suffer harm in this situation? In the law of negligence, the technical term for this is a duty of care.
- The second obvious legal issue (if Emily does have a duty of care to Caden) concerns how Emily should act in order to fulfil that duty given the circumstances she is facing. Emily knew that the man with the grenade was calm but might throw the grenade if provoked. Should she have worked out that, if the grenade were to be thrown, there would be devastation and that Caden as a haemophiliac would be at increased risk of serious injury? Emily chose to run – did fulfilling her duty of care to Caden legally require her to assess the situation differently and to make different choices? Could she be expected to have behaved any differently, given the circumstances she faced? In the law of negligence, the technical term for this is the standard of care.

The second step of the process is to work out how many research questions you need to create. Having carefully identified the relevant facts and the legal issues from the scenario, you are in a position to identify your research questions. You need to think about the most sensible way to group the various legal issues that you have identified. The following is a summary of how you could do this.

- These are two distinct issues. One relates to duty of care (is Emily responsible for Caden's injuries?), the other to standard of care (should/could Emily have behaved differently so as to prevent Caden's injuries?).
- These two distinct legal issues lend themselves to two distinct research questions – one dealing with duty of care, the other with standard of care.
- The first research question could be: 'Does Emily owe a duty of care to Caden?'
- The second research question could be: 'Did Emily meet the standard of care required to discharge her duty of care towards Caden, if one exists?'

The third step of the process is to work out the essential 'parts' of each research question. You have two research questions to deal with – answering them will require you to look at a number of different legal principles. You need to think carefully about what finer legal points you need to investigate for each question. The following is a summary of how you could do this.

- The first research question relates to whether Emily owes a duty of care to Caden. The first element of answering the research question is to identify the test for placing duties of care on individuals. If you know that this test consists of enquiring into the proximity of the parties, the foreseeability of the damage and public policy considerations, then the second element must be whether there was a proximate relationship between Emily and Caden. The third element must be whether Caden's injuries were a foreseeable result of Emily's decision to run from the sports complex, and whether there is anything that could break the chain of causation between Emily's decision and Caden's injuries. The fourth and final element must be whether there are any public policy considerations that could prevent Emily from owing a duty of care to Caden.
- The second research question relates to whether Emily met the required standard of care, if she is found to owe a duty of care to Caden. The first element of answering this research question is to identify the standard that is used to judge a defendant's actions in a situation in which they owe a duty of care to another person. Given that Emily was facing highly unusual circumstances, the second element could be whether there are any public policy or social utility considerations that would lower the standard of care that Emily must meet. The third element must, therefore, be whether Emily actually met the standard to be applied to her, given the known facts.

In summary: First, identify the key facts arising from the problem question scenario, and the key legal issues generated by those facts. Second, identify how many research questions you need to create, and what they should be. Third, work out the elements of each research question so that you can produce a satisfactory response to each question.

2.3 Planning the research required to answer your research question(s)

Once you have confirmed your research question(s), you will be ready to start doing the research itself. It is common for a law student to receive feedback that he or she has 'not discussed law that is relevant to the essay topic' or has 'not adopted a clear essay structure'. Naturally, this feedback may prompt several further questions.

- How do I decide what law is relevant to the question and what is not?
- How much of the relevant law do I need to talk about in my essay?
- What happens if I miss out some law that might be relevant?
- How do I figure out a good structure?

If you receive negative feedback relating to the content or structure of your essay, this may indicate that you need to improve the way that you plan your approach to your research question(s). This is also a key legal skill – without sufficient planning, your writing may not address the research question(s) accurately and could be difficult for a reader to follow. Irrelevant or unclear legal analysis can be worse than no analysis at all.

2.3.1 Prepare for planning by doing background reading

When you created your research question(s), you will have worked out their essential 'parts' or elements. Use these now to guide an initial period of background reading – this will help you to more effectively plan the detailed research required to answer your research question(s).

When conducting background reading you will read resources that give you a general overview of the relevant law. Secondary sources such as textbooks or practitioners' texts on the particular area of law are a good place to start. Doing this background reading before you start more targeted research allows you to familiarise yourself with the legal principles and literature that will be relevant to answering your research question(s). Importantly, it also allows you to begin formulating ideas and arguments on the topic and the research question(s). Good background reading should put you in a position to plan your targeted research.[5]

---

[5] Chris Hart provides an excellent summary of the importance of reviewing the secondary literature on your topic: 'without it you will not acquire

Background reading may seem straightforward; however, you should be wary of forming too rigid an opinion of the law during this stage of your research. The process of legal research involves forming plausible arguments about the law, testing those arguments, and then revising and supporting them based on what you have found. You should *not* set out with the objective of searching for information that confirms an argument that you want to make. Paying greater attention to information that confirms your ideas over information that disproves them is natural.[6] However, if you allow yourself to take an entrenched position on the law during your background reading, your detailed research will then become simply an exercise in mining information to support that position. Doing this does not serve any of the purposes of conducting legal research,[7] and may present an inaccurate and misleading analysis of your client's legal position.

You should, therefore, approach your background reading with the objective of gaining a broad awareness of the relevant law and literature, and of forming broad but *provisional* opinions on the legal issues at stake. Doing this will allow you to work out an argument that you *think* will be valid, but which you will plan to test with your more detailed reading. You must remain open to the possibility that, as you conduct your detailed research, the opinions you began to form during your background reading might have to change. Thus, the purpose of background reading can be summarised as putting you in a position to form your initial argument that you will later test and develop with your detailed research.

---

an understanding of your topic, know what has already been done on it, understand how it has been researched or grasp what the key issues are that need addressing. In your written project, you are expected to show that you understand previous research on your topic. You need to demonstrate that you understand the main theories used in your subject area, as well as how they have been applied and developed, and know what the main criticisms are of the research and method used in your field'. Chris Hart, *Doing a Literature Review: Releasing the Social Science Research Imagination* (2nd edn, Sage 2018), 2-3.

6   Confirmation bias is only one of a number of cognitive biases that lawyers should be aware that they are subject to. Awareness of these natural biases can help you to approach your research in a way that mitigates them to the greatest extent possible. For discussion, see: Joseph W Rand, 'Understanding Why Good Lawyers Go Bad: Using Case Studies in Teaching Cognitive Bias in Legal Decision-Making' (2003) 9 Clinical L Rev 731.

7   Mathias Siems and Daithí Mac Síthigh identify three purposes of legal research – research for the practical purpose of applying the law, research for the purpose of understanding the law itself, and research for the purpose of evaluating the utility and operation of law within society. None of these purposes would be served if you only seek to confirm ideas that you have, rather than test and refine those ideas based on what you find. Mathias M Siems and Daithí Mac Síthigh, 'Mapping Legal Research' (2012) 71 Cambridge Law Journal 651, 653–656.

> **Practical Tip:**
>
> You should do enough background reading so that you know enough to identify an initial argument that is plausible, but not so much that you become obsessed with a particular idea. Remember that your lecturers are asking you to construct arguments based on the facts, not to find facts that fit a particular argument.

As you conduct your background reading, keep a running list[8] of potentially relevant primary and other secondary sources that you come across in the text or footnotes. Highlight any of these sources that are referred to multiple times or which seem particularly useful or important. You can use this list to help you to decide what to read as part of your detailed research.

> **Example:**
>
> Consider the background reading you might do if you were faced with the scenario set out in Chapter 1 of this book.
>
> You know from the third step of the process of creating your research questions that you will need to conduct research on the law of negligence, specifically on the existence and discharge of duties of care. Some sources that you might go to first include the following.
>
> • The chapters on negligence in a general textbook on tort law. You can skip to the parts that specifically relate to duties of care.
> • Journal articles that discuss duties of care. You can look first at your tort law module reading list to see if any such articles are recommended. If not, you can do a general search on legal databases[9] for articles that discuss duties of care and standards of care within the context of negligence and tort law.
>
> Some examples of textbooks (which all contain chapters on negligence) that you could use for background reading include:
>
> • John Tully, *Tort Law in Ireland*;[10]
> • Bryan McMahon and William Binchy, *Law of Torts*;[11] or
> • Eoin Quill, *Torts in Ireland*.[12]

---

[8] Referencing software such as Microsoft Endnote can be helpful for organising the sources that you identify as relevant to your research question.

[9] Searching online legal databases is discussed in more detail in Chapter 3.

[10] John Tully, *Tort Law in Ireland* (Clarus 2014).

[11] Bryan McMahon and William Binchy, *Law of Torts* (4th edn, Bloomsbury 2013).

[12] Eoin Quill, *Torts in Ireland* (4th edn, Gill & Macmillan 2014).

In general, textbooks are the best option when conducting background reading. They are designed to provide accessible surveys of the relevant law and principles, and are written specifically for readers who want an introduction to the subject and a starting point from which to launch their research. Even experienced academics and legal practitioners rely on subject textbooks if they need to conduct research in a field of law with which they are unfamiliar, or they want to revisit how the basic tenets and principles of their specialist field are presented to the outside world.

While textbooks are an excellent resource for background reading, academic journal articles can also be a useful resource at this stage. Look first at those that have been recommended by your lecturer on your module reading list. Then search online legal databases for journal articles of general relevance to your topic, which could provide you with some introductory insights.

For example:

- Steve Hedley, 'Making sense of negligence';[13] or
- William Binchy, 'Tort Law in Ireland: A Half-Century Review'.[14]

These journal articles are theoretical in nature, but they offer a general overview of negligence and Irish tort law respectively. They could provide a helpful orientation for a law student who is completely new to tort law, and who is seeking more detailed explanation of its foundational ideas.

It would not make sense to search for specific cases as part of your background reading. You are trying first to establish the two tests relating to duties of care and standards of care – the first element of each question. You need to read at a general level for this by using textbooks and journal articles. As a result, your background reading should be dedicated to making yourself familiar with the elements of each research question. When you have done this, you will be in a position to then identify the specific cases, academic literature and other sources that you will need to read in detail in order to research how the elements of the research questions (that is, the different elements of the duty of care and standard of care tests) should be addressed in detail.

Remember that the purpose of your background reading is to form a broad awareness of the law involved in answering the research question, and to form initial ideas and arguments. For the scenario set out in Chapter 1 of this book, first you need to make yourself aware of the legal principles involved in addressing each element of your two research questions and form an argument (based on your initial reading and your understanding of the facts) about how those principles might apply to Emily and Caden's situation. You will then plan detailed reading to discover whether your argument is correct.

---

[13] Steve Hedley, 'Making sense of negligence' (2016) 36(3) Legal Studies 491.
[14] William Binchy, 'Tort Law in Ireland: A Half-Century Review' (2016) 56 The Irish Jurist 199.

2.3.2 Good research planning – preparing for your detailed research

If you conduct your background research correctly, you will be in a good position to plan your detailed research. Detailed research involves reading more targeted secondary sources (such as topic-specific books) and primary sources.

There are, therefore, two things that your background reading should enable you to plan:
- a specific 'proposed' argument; and
- a list of the most relevant source types that you will need to search for and read in detail in order to test your proposed argument.

These will help you to focus your detailed research on information that is most relevant to testing and revising your initial ideas about the law, and which will lead you to an accurate, relevant and clear response to your research question(s).

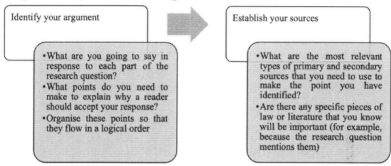

Identifying your potential argument: A question that you will face in legal writing is how to build a potential argument that responds to your research question(s) and is persuasive. This is a difficult legal writing skill to master – it will take practice before you find it easy to plan out persuasive arguments.

Building a persuasive argument involves explaining clearly and logically how and why the law should be understood to apply or function in a particular way and providing evidence to support these explanations.[15] A persuasive argument expresses your opinion about how the research question(s) should be answered. Thus, building a persuasive argument does not involve simply presenting the law or regurgitating the facts with which you have

---

[15] For an in-depth examination of how to build effective legal arguments, see for example: James A Gardner, *Legal Argument: The Structure and Language of Effective Advocacy* (2nd edn, Lexis Nexis 2007).

been presented. This is the case whether you are writing an essay for a lecturer or providing a letter of advice for a client – anyone can read a textbook to find out what the law is on a particular point. You will need to analyse the law, as it applies to the facts, and provide evidence to support your conclusions (which could include case law and legislation, as well as what other authorities in the field have said).

Once you are comfortable with the fact that you must do more than just describe the law, you will be able to plan a strong initial argument based on your background reading. To do so, you must be honest with yourself and clear for your readers – honest with what you have actually found through your background reading, and clear in how you are going to communicate the argument that you have formulated to an audience that does not have the benefit of sharing your internal thought processes.[16]

- **Honesty with yourself**
  - o What does your background reading objectively tell you about the law? What are the arguments that you could plausibly make, and what does the initial evidence you have seen actually suggest?
  - o What do you think about the law, based on your background reading? Do not feel compelled to think what others think or think what you assume your reader wants to hear.
  - o What evidence will contradict your provisional argument? You will need to investigate and address counter arguments, so you cannot ignore contrary evidence.

- **Clarity for your readers**
  - o Ensure that you convey your argument in plain and clear steps that are not too complex to understand for a reader who might not have any knowledge of the specific essay topic.
  - o Ensure that you organise the stages of your argument in a way that makes sense to outside readers, not just in a way that makes sense to you.
  - o Ensure that your argument, through its individual stages, conveys a plain and clear overarching message that your readers will be able to follow as they read what you have written.

---

16 Academics have explored how the style of your writing can make your legal analysis even more effective and persuasive. See for example: Sean Flammer, 'Persuading Judges: An Empirical Analysis of Writing Style, Persuasion, and the Use of Plain English' (2010) 16 Legal Writing: J Legal Writing Inst 183.

Establishing your detailed sources: Identifying the most relevant sources to read in greater depth is a difficult skill to master, and it will take a lot of practise before you become comfortable in deciding which sources and points of analysis are the most relevant to answering a research question.[17] This is largely because it takes confidence to decide that a piece of information is not immediately relevant to your legal writing objectives and to disregard it.

You may notice that you sometimes receive feedback from lecturers that 'your work is too descriptive'. This indicates that you have spent too much of your essay trying to describe all the information that you found about the subject of your essay, and have probably included more information than is necessary to answer the research question(s) effectively. Your lecturer is indicating that you should instead spend more time analysing and applying the law that is *specifically relevant* to the research question(s). Once you internalise this fact, you will become increasingly comfortable with the idea that it is acceptable—indeed, that it is essential—to leave out information that might be generally important within the topic, but which is not immediately relevant to the particular question(s) that you are trying to answer.

You can then start to build confidence in the way you plan your detailed reading. You must be confident in the reasons why the sources you are choosing to read in detail are relevant, and discerning in ignoring the sources that you consider to be irrelevant. How then do you decide what is relevant and irrelevant? The following graphic summarises some advice for making this decision.

> Does the argument that you are constructing rely on this source to be successful? Is the information in the source essential or just interesting?

> Is this source duplicating the examples already provided by other sources?

> Does the source provide background or context that is not essential to successfully answering the question?

> Does the source relate to a state of the law that is outdated?

---

[17] This skill is a part of what has been called 'information literacy' in the literature. There are varying definitions of this term – essentially it means the ability to find information, decide whether it is relevant to your work, and decide how to use it within your work. For further discussion of the importance of building information literacy skills as a law student, see for example: Ellie Margolis and Kristen E Murray, 'Say Goodbye to the Books: Information Literacy as the New Legal Research Paradigm' (2012) 38 University of Dayton Law Review 117.

Example:

Faced with the scenario set out in Chapter 1 of this book, **first, you plan your argument**.

Imagine that you have gained the following basic insights about the duty of care and standard of care tests from your background reading.

- The existence of a duty of care is determined by the proximity of the parties, the foreseeability of the damage and any public policy considerations.
- A defendant can only be held liable for a plaintiff's injuries if his/her actions can be concretely linked to those injuries.
- A *novus actus interveniens* can prevent a defendant from being held liable for a plaintiff's injuries. It is an act outside the defendant's control that breaks the chain of causation.
- The standard of care that a person bearing a duty of care must meet is an objective standard. It is what a reasonable person would do or not do in the circumstances faced by the defendant. The standard of care cannot be determined subjectively by thinking about whether the defendant acted to the best of his or her abilities and judgment.
- The context in which the defendant acted can alter the assessment of whether their actions were reasonable – in particular, where the defendant's actions have high social utility or where the defendant acted in particularly pressured circumstances, the assessment of what actions are reasonable can be more lenient.

From this, you might arrive at the following *potential* arguments in response to the research questions.

- First, the question about duty of care. Emily and Caden were clearly proximate. It is possible that Emily could not have foreseen that Caden would kick the display of tennis rackets as they ran, or that the shattered glass would hit Caden and cause him to bleed. However, Emily should have foreseen that running from the sports complex with a young child in highly pressured circumstances might be likely to create some level of noise, which would alert the armed men to their presence. She should also have foreseen that, if the armed men were alerted to two people running from the sports complex, they would carry out their threat of violence. Since Emily knew about Caden's haemophilia, she should then have foreseen that violence might be likely to lead to Caden sustaining an injury from which he would bleed uncontrollably. Moreover, when the man with the grenade threw it towards Emily and Caden, this could not be an intervening act, because it cannot be considered outside of Emily's control – in fact the man made clear that he would detonate the grenade if anyone in the area moved. Finally, there are no policy reasons that would cause you to hesitate to impose a duty of care on Emily. Thus, your first potential argument could be that Emily did owe a duty of care to Caden.
- Second, the question about standard of care. Since the standard of care is objective, then you cannot argue that Emily should not be held liable

because she did what she thought was right in order to protect Caden. Indeed, it is probable that she is liable because she did not act in the manner that a reasonable person would have under the circumstances. She and Caden were hidden from the armed men, she knew that Caden had haemophilia, and the man with the grenade stated that he would detonate it if anyone moved. Against these circumstances, the reasonable person in Emily's position would have stayed where he or she was. A reasonable person would have calculated that avoiding provoking the armed men by running would be more likely to avoid serious harm coming to Caden, whose life could be put at risk by even the most minor of injuries. A reasonable person would have calculated that, even if he or she decided to run, the likelihood of making some noise and alerting the men to their presence was high. Furthermore, a reasonable person would have calculated that, even if they did run, and the men did notice their presence, the man with the grenade would be likely to detonate it and that severe injuries would likely result from this. Thus, your second potential argument could be that Emily fell below the standard of care that she owed to Caden.

Second, you plan your detailed sources. Given the provisional arguments you have planned above, you might select the following sources for more detailed reading in order to test that argument.

Cases – clearly, testing your arguments will rely heavily upon close reading and application of relevant case law. Here are some of the cases that you could plan to read in detail:

- *Ward v McMaster*[18] – this case sets out the test for the existence of a duty of care.
- *Hayes v Minister for Finance*;[19] *Breslin v Corcoran*[20] – these cases establish the circumstances in which a third-party action cannot be considered a *novus actus interveniens*.
- *Home Office v Dorset Yacht Co*[21] – this case discusses how defendants should guard against the tortious or criminal acts of third parties.
- *Breslin v Brennan*[22] – this case discusses the standard of care to be expected of a defendant where the risk of injury to a child is at issue.
- *O'Neill v Dunnes Stores*[23] – this case establishes the test for the objective standard of care.
- *McComiskey v McDermott*[24] – this case establishes that the objective standard of care must be determined according to the circumstances of the case.
- *Daborn v Bath Tramways Motor Co Ltd & T Rogersey*[25] – this case

---

[18] *Ward v McMaster* [1988] IR 337.
[19] *Hayes v Minister for Finance* [2007] 3 IR 190.
[20] *Breslin v Corcoran* [2003] 2 IR 203.
[21] *Home Office v Dorset Yacht Co* [1970] AC 1004.
[22] *Breslin v Brennan* [1937] IR 350.
[23] *O'Neill v Dunnes Stores* [2010] IESC 53.
[24] *McComiskey v McDermott* [1974] IR 75.
[25] *Daborn v Bath Tramways Motor Co & T Rogersey* [1946] 2 All ER 333.

establishes that the standard of care may take into account the ultimate purpose of the defendant's actions, and whether they served an important purpose.

- *O'Donovan v Cork Co Council*[26] – this case establishes that the standard of care may take into account any need for urgent action in the defendant's situation, and whether the defendant could have been expected to act differently if he or she had enjoyed more time to think.

Books and Journal Articles – to test your arguments, you will not only need to read the applicable law in detail, you will also need to consider the arguments of others on how this law could be applied in similar circumstances. Given that you need to think closely about how Emily should have acted in light of the fact that she was the responsible adult in charge of a youth sports team, you could take a closer look at the following:

- Neil Partington, 'Sports coaching and the law of negligence: implications for coaching practice'[27] – although this article mostly focuses on negligence committed when engaging in coaching itself, it could be useful to help you establish a sense of the extent to which volunteer coaches should be aware of, and understand, the legal duties of care placed upon individuals in their position. This could help you to assess the state of mind and thought processes that should have been expected of Emily when she realised that she and Caden were in a dangerous situation.
- Laura Donnellan and Susan Leahy, *Sports Law in Ireland*[28] – this book discusses several aspects of the law that are not relevant to your research questions, but it does contain some discussion on negligence liability of sports coaches in Ireland. As a fairly rare example of Irish academic work containing analysis of the Irish law that is directly relevant to the situation in your scenario, it is worth examining in more detail.
- Neil Partington, '*Murray v McCullough (as Nominee on Behalf of the Trustees and on Behalf of the Board of Governors of Rainey Endowed School)* [2016] NIQB 52'[29] – this case note discusses a situation involving the liability of a schoolteacher for sports injuries sustained to a pupil under her care who was playing a hockey match. Although this is not exactly analogous to the situation in your scenario, and although the case was decided by the High Court of Northern Ireland with reference to case law of England and Wales, the article does discuss key principles relevant to determining whether a legal duty of care is placed upon an adult who assumes temporary responsibility for the care of children, which does capture the situation of a volunteer coach in charge of a sports team outing. The discussion in this case note could, therefore, help you in analysing how the relevant principles of Irish law should apply to Emily.

---

[26] *O'Donovan v Cork Co Council* [1967] IR 173.
[27] Neil Partington, 'Sports coaching and the law of negligence: implications for coaching practice' (2017) 6(1) Sports Coaching Review 36.
[28] Laura Donnellan and Susan Leahy, *Sports Law in Ireland* (2nd edn, Kluwer 2017).
[29] Neil Partington, '*Murray v McCullough (as Nominee on Behalf of the Trustees and*

Why should you bother to plan your research in this manner, especially if you are only doing a short essay for which you do not have a lot of time? There are several reasons.

- You give yourself the best chance of producing a piece of writing that responds to the research question(s). If you dive straight into detailed reading without thinking first about what you are reading, you will be far more likely to waste time reading things that are not relevant to producing an effective answer to your research question(s). In turn, you will be more likely to write about that irrelevant information. If this happens, you may also struggle to cut out words at the end of the writing process to meet any maximum word count.
- You give yourself the best chance of addressing all of the important legal issues. Many questions that your lecturers set are designed to have more than one 'layer' to them – they are designed to test how well you can identify and address not only the most obvious legal issues in a given scenario, but also the more nuanced issues. If you do not take the time to look carefully at a research question in order to identify the possible layers of legal issues and the best way to address them, you will end up producing a piece of writing that only provides partial, and potentially incorrect, legal analysis.
- You give yourself the best chance of organising your work in a clear and logical manner. Even the shortest and most straightforward pieces of legal writing will require you to work through a number of points of legal analysis to produce a satisfactory answer. If you start writing without considering the order in which you are going to present your points, you will be leaving the clarity of your writing down to luck. The order in which you personally think of, and write down, your points may not be an order that makes sense to other people who read your work. By planning your approach to answering the research question(s), you can ensure that you will present your legal analysis in an order that is most likely to be clear and make sense to others.

---

on Behalf of the Board of Governors of Rainey Endowed School) [2016] NIQB 52' (2016) 67 Northern Ireland Legal Quarterly 251.

Practical Tip:

Everybody has a slightly different learning style, which means that they also have a different planning style. Some students plan well with lists, others with diagrams, etc. Employ the planning style that works best for you. Although drawing inspiration from your peers can be very helpful, if you have established a way of planning that works well for you, do not feel that you must change it simply because you see your peers doing something different.

2.4 Chapter summary

- Every piece of legal research begins with one or more research questions. Read your assignment brief carefully, and identify suitable research questions to guide your work. Identifying at least one suitable research question is essential if you want to produce well-defined, focussed and clearly structured work.

- Do some background reading on the topic of each research question before you start planning, but be careful not to form entrenched ideas on how a research question should be answered at this stage.

- Plan the provisional argument that you think you can make in response to each research question. This planned argument will be tested with your detailed research. Remember to be honest with yourself and clear for your readers when planning your argument.

- Identify sources for detailed research that are most relevant to each research question and planned argument. Remember that you need to support your argument with relevant information. Including lots of information that is irrelevant to your research question will weaken your argument. Be confident in deciding what is relevant, and discerning in ignoring what is irrelevant.

Chapter 3

Finding Information

Having planned out the sources that you need to read in detail in order to answer your research question(s), you will now need to find these sources.

Being an effective and efficient researcher takes more than simply knowing how to operate the relevant legal databases, although this is of course a big part of it. You should also be familiar with the nature and utility of the different sources that you are searching for, as well as how to extract and record the information that you need from these sources.

3.1 Types of legal sources

Certain types of legal sources will be essential for you, as a legal researcher. Acts of the Oireachtas (also known as statutes), cases decided by the Irish courts, and books and journal articles written by academics about Irish law might all spring immediately to mind. However, many other types of sources will be relevant to your work and will become increasingly relevant as your legal research becomes more complex.

You should try to familiarise yourself with the range of sources that you have available to you so that you know where to find them and you know how to cite them.

There are a number of core legal sources for a researcher in Ireland.

Primary sources	
European Union ('EU') legislation and case law	• EU legislation and case law are relevant to a number of different subjects, not just EU law itself. • EU Regulations[1] and Directives[2] set out common rules for Ireland and the other EU Member States. • EU Decisions are legal acts taken jointly or individually by EU institutions.[3] • While Recommendations and Opinions of EU institutions are not binding on EU Member States, they may still be helpful as part of your research.
Irish Constitution	• The Irish Constitution (or Bunreacht na hÉireann) is the supreme domestic law of the Irish State and takes precedence over inferior sources of Irish law. • It is relevant across many subjects of Irish law, in particular anything dealing with the administration of state or rights of citizens. • Subject to a small number of exceptions, all Irish law must be consistent with the Irish Constitution.
Irish legislation	• Irish legislation is likely to be relevant to most subjects of Irish law that you are researching. • Legislation takes precedence over case law in the hierarchy of sources of Irish law. • Primary legislation (statutes) is enacted by the Oireachtas. Secondary or delegated legislation (such as Statutory Instruments) are measures enacted by bodies or persons to whom the Oireachtas has delegated certain law-making powers.

---

[1] Regulations are legally binding instruments enacted by the institutions of the EU. From the date of their entry into force, Regulations have immediate and direct effect in EU Member States.

[2] Like Regulations, Directives are legally binding instruments enacted by the institutions of the EU. Unlike Regulations, Directives are only binding as to their ultimate result, rather than the mechanism for achieving that result in individual EU Member States.

[3] Where an EU Decision has specific addressees, it will bind those addressees. If the addressee of an EU Decision is one or more specified Member States, individuals within those Member States may invoke rights or obligations created by the EU Decision before national courts (but only against the Member State).

Irish case law	<ul><li>Irish case law is likely to be a rich source of information for your research.</li><li>When reading case law as part of your research, always make a note of which court delivered the judgment – decisions of courts of superior jurisdiction will be a more authoritative statement of the law than decisions of courts of lower jurisdiction.</li></ul>
Other sources	
International treaties and tribunals	<ul><li>International treaties and the decisions of international tribunals will be relevant to several different subjects, not just public international law.</li><li>Remember, an international agreement (such as a treaty or convention) does not become part of Irish law until it is incorporated into Irish law (for example, the European Convention on Human Rights was incorporated into Irish law by the European Convention of Human Rights Act 2003).</li><li>With respect to the jurisprudence of international courts – Ireland has undertaken to abide by final decisions of the European Court of Human Right in cases to which Ireland is a party.[4]</li></ul>
Foreign case law	<ul><li>Subject to the above, an Irish court is not bound to follow the decision of a foreign court.</li><li>However, decisions of foreign courts could be very relevant to your research, particularly if your research includes a comparative element.</li><li>If you are referring to the decisions of foreign courts, always make a note of which court delivered the judgment.</li></ul>
Secondary sources	
Legislative debates	<ul><li>Records of the debates held in the Dáil and the Seanad can be a useful source of information.</li><li>These records provide an analysis of Acts that have been enacted and Bills that are being considered for enactment.</li><li>Legislative debates can tell you the factors that led to certain provisions being included or excluded, or tell you the political motivations for passing or not passing certain legislation.</li></ul>

---

[4] European Convention on Human Rights, Art 46.

Reports	• Reports are produced by government departments, statutory bodies, executive agencies, expert groups, international organisations and non-governmental organisations (NGOs).
	• They are documents that assess and comment on the law and legislative reform options.
	• Reports are useful for examining whether the law is working as expected, and the desirability of, and rationale for, legal reform proposals.
Books and journal articles	• Books and journal articles written by academics and practitioners can be an invaluable resource in your research.
	• Books and journal articles are not sources of Irish law, but are useful in helping you to understand complex legal principles.
Newspapers, blogs, and websites	• Academic work is not the only source of commentary on the law – journalistic work can also provide valuable legal commentary.
	• Newspapers, blogs and websites are particularly useful when the legal issue under consideration has only emerged very recently or develops extremely rapidly, and academic commentary has not yet been produced on it.
	• Care must be exercised with these sources though – they are more likely to be written from a biased or heavily opinionated viewpoint, and less likely to be rigorously researched or referenced.
	• Some of these sources may be more reliable than others – quality daily newspapers (and their online versions) and websites maintained by governments and international NGOs can be a good source of information.

Evidence from scientific, political, economic, sociological and similar fields	• Lawyers may need to support their legal arguments with evidence from other fields of study. • At third level, you may be asked to do socio-legal research[5] – this will require you to draw upon information outside of the legal field in order to write persuasive analyses of the law. • It is, therefore, a good idea to read widely to expose yourself to academic work from non-legal disciplines, so that you have a sense of the value and relevance of such work to legal issues, and know how to read and interpret such work.

Practical Tip:

The main message from this chapter is that there are a number of different sources that you will have to draw upon as part of your legal research, other than just statutes, case law, and the occasional book or journal article. Your ability to work with alternative source types will improve vastly if you devote some attention to becoming familiar with as broad a range of sources as possible, as soon as possible.

It is helpful for legal researchers to think about the available sources of information as belonging to one of two classes: primary sources or secondary sources.

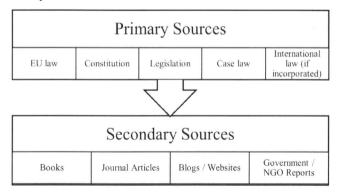

Primary Sources				
EU law	Constitution	Legislation	Case law	International law (if incorporated)

Secondary Sources			
Books	Journal Articles	Blogs / Websites	Government / NGO Reports

---

5   There are various methods of conducting legal research – for further explanation, see: Chris Dent 'A Law Student-Oriented Taxonomy for Research in Law' (2017) 48 Victoria University of Wellington Law Review 371. The socio-legal method is one in which the legal researcher investigates how law 'shapes and is shaped by broader social, political and economic logics, contexts and relations': Darren O'Donovan, 'Socio-Legal Methodology: Conceptual Underpinnings, Justifications and Practical Pitfalls' in Laura Cahillane and Jennifer Schweppe (eds), *Legal Research Methods: Principles and Practicalities* (Clarus Press 2016).

(1) **Primary sources:** Think of primary sources as 'the law'. These sources include EU Directives and Regulations, EU case law, the Irish Constitution, Irish legislation, Irish case law, international treaties (where incorporated into Irish law), and international cases (where Ireland is a party). These sources contain the legal rules that lawyers need to apply in order to answer the legal research question(s) they have identified.

(2) **Secondary sources:** Think of secondary sources as 'commentary on the law'. These include academic books and journal articles, blogs and reports. They are not 'the law' – they do not contain the legal rules that we need to find and apply in order to resolve a legal research question. What they do is offer analysis, perspective and insight on how the rules could or should be interpreted and reformed.

The following are the main things to remember when working with different legal sources.

- **If you want to discuss what the law is, you should read and cite primary sources of law.** Do not rely only on reading excerpts of legislation or cases in a book or journal article. While you can (and should) use books and journal articles to conduct background reading to make yourself familiar with the relevant primary sources, if you want to understand what the current law actually is, you must read the primary sources that contain it.

> **Example:**
>
> When conducting your research for the scenario used in this book, you will want to know the main principles of how duties of care arise. To do so, you will need to go and read the leading Irish cases on duties of care *in full* during your detailed research stage. Do not simply try to find out what these cases say by reading more books and journal articles that discuss them – this will not be enough detail and you may miss something important in the primary sources.

- **If you want help forming opinions and arguments about the law, or you want help guiding you to the primary sources of that law, you should read and cite secondary sources**. Academic books and journal articles can help you to think about whether the law contained in primary sources is effective, whether it is ethical, how it has developed, and what options exist for reforming it. If you read an extract from a statute or a case in a book or a journal article, you should always read and then cite the statute or case itself as the source of the extract. Quite often, students will cite secondary sources in which they read extracts of primary sources as if the secondary source was the original source of that extract. This is wrong and suggests that you have not read the relevant primary source. When you want to discuss a primary source, always go and find that primary source and ensure that you have cited it correctly in your legal writing.

Moreover, when you are working with secondary sources that make reference to other secondary sources, you should always try to cite the original source of an idea, explanation or argument. You will quite often read quotations in books or articles that are taken from another academic book or article. Ideally, you should go and find the cited material itself and read the section of it in which the quotation that you like is located – you may well find further information that is helpful to you. You then cite the original source of the quotation in your legal writing.[6] See Chapter 6 for more information on citing primary and secondary sources.

3.2 Identifying the correct databases and constructing effective search queries

Now it is time to discuss how you find sources of legal information, using libraries, online legal databases and other general search engines. First though, you should briefly consider the nature of the search tools that you will be working with.

Today, many legal sources can be accessed online – indeed, an increasing number of printed books also exist in e-book format, and most Irish universities will have purchased the e-book versions of the core textbooks and other relevant monographs and edited collections. As a result, although it is still an excellent idea to go to the law section of your institution's library and spend some time browsing through the collections that are relevant to the subject that you are researching, much of the information that you will need to access in order to research successfully can be accessed through online databases and search engines. In particular, due to the digitisation of the legislative and case law reporting processes,

---

6   This is discussed in detail in Section 6.2.5 below.

you do not necessarily need to look at printed law reports or printed legislation – you can find the primary sources you need to work with far more quickly and accurately by searching online.

While search engines like Google are a useful tool for conducting legal research, they are still only tools, not magic wands.[7] They will only perform as designed and as directed – as will any other database that you use. Google searches the whole of the internet for the search terms you input. This means that, unless you are looking for a specific source with very specific search terms, Google will return a vast number of results from all over the internet that match your search terms. The majority of these results will not be the relevant information that you are searching for and the piece of information that you do want may be buried amongst all the other results. It is no surprise, therefore, that if you use Google to search generally for sources of legal information, or to search for a specific source for which you have incomplete information (perhaps a case name, or a journal article title, but not the full case or article citation), a mass of irrelevant results may lead you to think that the information you want does not exist. This may not be true. In the vast number of research situations, the information that you want will be out there somewhere. If you cannot find it at first, this simply means that you are looking in the wrong place, using the wrong search tools, using the wrong search terms, or just are not looking through your search results carefully enough.

You need to ensure that you are using the right database when you search for sources of legal information and that you use it in an effective manner. This means being aware of what each database contains, how to use its search functions, and how to design search queries that are most likely to return relevant results.

3.2.1 Irish legislation

The easiest way to find and read Irish statutes is through the Electronic Irish Statute Book database (eISB) (**www. irishstatutebook.ie**). This is a freely available database. Simply type the name and date of the Act or Statutory Instrument you are searching for into the search box.

---

[7]   Academics have examined the expectations of the so-called 'Google generation' – those who have grown up with technology and the internet as integral parts of their lives – when it comes to finding sources of information. See, for example: Daniel Bates, 'Are "Digital Natives" Equipped to Conquer the Legal Landscape?' (University of Cambridge Faculty of Law Research Paper No 26/2013); Ian Gallacher, '"Forty-Two:" A Hitchhikers Guide To Teaching Legal Research To The Google Generation' (2006) 39 Akron Law Review 151.

The Law Reform Commission website (**www.lawreform.ie**) is also a helpful freely available database. It includes a database of consolidated legislation under the 'Revised Acts' tab. This includes all Acts of the Oireachtas since 2006 that have subsequently been amended as well as frequently used pre-2006 Acts. Consolidated legislation can be searched for chronologically or alphabetically.

Most Irish third-level institutions where law is taught will subscribe to the Westlaw database. This is an all-purpose specialised legal database that allows you to search for legislation, case law, academic articles and legal news. Your institution may subscribe to both Westlaw IE (**www.westlaw.ie**) and Westlaw UK (**www.westlaw.co.uk**). If you are looking for Irish legislation and related commentary, then you need to use the Irish version of Westlaw. If you are looking for United Kingdom or EU law, use Westlaw UK. Since Westlaw is a subscription-based database, you generally cannot access it freely online. Instead, you will need to access Westlaw IE and Westlaw UK through your institution's library.

To find Irish legislation on Westlaw IE, simply click on the 'Legislation' tab, then type the name and date of the Act or Statutory Instrument that you are looking for.

3.2.2 Irish case law

The Courts Service of Ireland website (**www.courts.ie**) holds transcripts of judgments delivered by the Irish courts since 2001. While these transcripts do not contain headnotes, the Courts Service of Ireland website can be very useful when searching for recent cases that have not yet been published in a law report. You can search by keyword, court, judge, citation or date. This website is freely available.

BAILII (**www.bailii.org**) is a freely available website that contains judgments from Irish cases heard in the High Court, Court of Appeal and Supreme Court. These judgments do not contain headnotes. Cases can be searched for using the simple search function or you can browse by year. BAILII also contains other Irish legal resources such as legislation.

Westlaw IE can also be used to search for Irish case law. When you click on the 'Cases' tab, you will be presented with a new set of search boxes.

- If you are searching for a specific case, and you have a

full law report or neutral citation for it,[8] type the citation into the citation box.

- If you just have the names of the parties and also know the subject matter of the case, type those into the relevant boxes.

Be careful to select the judgment you actually want when you are presented with the search results. Cases in the same line of litigation could have been heard in multiple courts. Also, bear in mind that the main Irish law reports (that is, the Irish Reports or the Irish Law Reports Monthly) could amalgamate the judgment from the lower court in which a case was first heard with the judgment from a superior appeal court within the one report.

Example:

Imagine that, as part of the detailed research that you need to do in relation to Emily and Caden's fact pattern, you are trying to find the Supreme Court decision in the case of *Ward v McMaster*, which you know is about the existence of a duty of care. You decide to use Westlaw IE.

After typing the party names into the relevant search box, you are presented with two results: one for *Dennis Ward and Anne Ward v Patrick McMaster, Louth County Council and Nicholas Hardy and Company* [1989] ILRM 400; the other for *Denis Ward and Anne Ward v Patrick McMaster, Louth County Council and Nicholas Hardy and Co Ltd* [1986] ILRM 43. You will notice that both have virtually the same name, but have different dates. The first result is the one that you need – if you look carefully at the result listings, you will see that this is the Supreme Court's judgment on the case. The second result, with the earlier date, is the judgment from the High Court where the case was initially brought. Ensure that when your search returns very similar results, you look at those results carefully and select the one that you need.

Westlaw IE is not the only legal database in which you can search for Irish case law. Indeed, sometimes you may find that Westlaw IE does not hold a report of the case that you are looking for. Unlike Google, which searches all of the internet, specialised legal databases like Westlaw IE have finite content, even if that content is very large. Thus, although a specialised legal database should be the first place to look for specific legal sources, you need to be aware that they have limits in terms of content. You may at some point hit that limit, and this is true not just for case law, but

---

[8] See Section 6.3.1 below for more details on how to cite case law.

for legislation, academic journal articles and so on. When you cannot find the case or journal article that you are looking for, do not immediately assume that it does not exist – you may simply have reached the content limits of the particular database you are searching in. If this is the case, rather than give up you need to try a different database.

Fortunately, multiple legal databases exit in which you can find case law. Most Irish universities and other third-level institutions will also subscribe to JustisOne (**app.justis.com**). JustisOne is transitioning to a new platform, vLex Justis, in the course of 2021. JustisOne can be used to find legislation and case law from the United Kingdom, Ireland, the EU and a range of common law countries. JustisOne has an 'all-in-one' simple search function, which makes it a user-friendly alternative to Westlaw IE. This database also gives you an overview of the status of cases – if you click the 'Overview' link above each case, this will set out the main categories of legal research that are relevant to the case and extracts of those passages from the case that have been most frequently cited. The other links above each case provide details of cases cited in the judgment, legislation that has been relied on in the judgment and the treatment of the case in subsequent cases.

Example:

Imagine that you are now trying to find the Supreme Court judgment in *Breslin v Brennan*, which you know relates to the objective standard of care in negligence and what a reasonable person would have done in the defendant's circumstances (let us imagine for the sake of this example that you only know the party names, and the subject matter – this can often be the case if lecturers mention cases in class, without providing the citation). You might try searching first on Westlaw IE, typing the names of the parties into the relevant search box. You will find that no results are returned. This indicates that Westlaw IE does not contain the case report that you are looking for.

Therefore, you must try another database. Searching on JustisOne proves to be more fruitful. Typing the names of the parties into the simple search function (or into the relevant box in the detailed advance search function, which works like the search functions in Westlaw IE) returns several results, the first of which matches the party names you have searched for. Clicking on the case name takes you to the judgment and related overview information. Here, you will be able to see from the keywords listed at the start of the case report that you have found the information that you are looking for.

For many students, the simple search function in JustisOne is a powerful tool. The 'Free Text' search function in Westlaw IE performs a similar (but probably slightly less effective) job. However, when using these search functions, remember that the database is more likely to return many more irrelevant results, especially if you are not searching for one case in particular, but rather any case that is relevant to a certain topic or list of keywords.

If you use the simple search or Free Text search functions, you must look through your search results carefully. Sift out those cases that are relevant to your work and those which are not.

> **Practical Tip:**
>
> Explore both Westlaw IE and JustisOne to decide which one you would prefer to use as your go-to database for case law.

3.2.3 EU and ECHR sources

In many ways, searching for legal sources connected to the EU and ECHR legal orders is straightforward. This is because the relevant databases are freely available online – you can access them by searching for them with Google and you will not have to search in a specialised legal database that can only be accessed through your institution's library.

The EUR-LEX database (**eur-lex.europa.eu/homepage.html**) enables you to access EU Treaties, Regulations, Directives and other legislation. On the website you will be able to use the quick search function to search for a specific piece of legislation (simply type in the name of the legislation, or, even better, its Official Journal reference if you know this), or browse legislation by topic.

Although the EUR-LEX database allows you to search for EU case law, the Court of Justice of the European Union has its own database – CURIA (**curia.europa.eu/juris**). This is far more useful for finding EU case law. On the website you can search for specific cases using the party names, case number, or ECLI (European Case Law Identifier) reference. If you are searching for relevant case law on a certain topic, you can use the 'Text' search function to search for keywords or phrases. This is similar to the Westlaw IE 'Free Text' search function, or the JustisOne simple search function.

The European Court of Human Rights also has a specific database for its case law – HUDOC (**hudoc.echr.coe.int**). You can search for case law using party names and case references using the simple search bar at the top of the screen or by clicking on the link to the 'Advanced Search' function.

3.2.4 Academic literature

Your first port of call when searching for books and journal articles should always be your institution's library. The majority of third-level institution libraries will hold extensive collections of printed law books and will subscribe to a range of legal databases. While you might find it helpful to browse your library's printed collections, it is often more efficient to first search for academic literature using your library's online catalogue.

Whatever you are searching for, you should start with the simple search function presented to you on the library home page, if one exists.

(1) **Books:** If you search for a book using your library catalogue's simple search function, you may receive a number of results. These might include various editions of the book, reviews of the book and books with a similar name to the book. If there are multiple editions of a book held in your library, you will typically want to access the most recent edition.

When you locate the book that you want in the search results, review the relevant result page to see if your library holds a physical copy of the book (if it does, make a note of the shelf location) and/or an electronic version of the book.

> **Example:**
>
> Imagine that, as part of your research on Emily and Caden's fact pattern, you are searching for McMahon and Binchy's *Law of Torts*. Using the simple search function of Maynooth University's library catalogue (by way of example) to search for the title of the book, you will see that the library holds a physical copy of the book at location 344.17063MCM. By going to this location in the library, you will be able to find the physical copy of the book. You will see from the search results that no electronic version of this book is held by the library.

(2) **Journal articles:** The same process can be used to find academic journal articles. You can find specific journal articles in the same way as you would find specific books – if the library holds a subscription to the journal in which the article is published, it will return the relevant result to you.

If you are searching for journal articles on a topic more

generally, limit the search of your library's catalogue to journal articles and use the simple search bar to search for relevant keywords. This will help you to pinpoint the topic that you are searching for articles on.

Your institution's library is a good place to start your search for journal articles.[9] However, the list of journals that your library subscribes to directly will not be endless. This is why libraries will nearly always subscribe to several specific online legal databases, which themselves will hold large collections of law journals. If you cannot find what you are looking for using your institution's library, try searching for it in the legal databases that your library subscribes to. Your library's website will most likely have a list of databases to which it subscribes.

There are a number of subscription-based legal databases that your library might subscribe to:

(a) **Westlaw IE:** The Westlaw IE database includes a wide selection of Irish academic and practitioner journals. Navigate to the 'Journals' tab on the database. You can use the 'Free Text' search bar to search for articles on a given topic. However, if you are looking for a specific article you can enter the title and/or author of the article in the relevant search boxes.

(b) **LexisLibrary (www.lexisnexis.com):** LexisLibrary is a United Kingdom centred database and contains a comprehensive list of full-text journal articles and books from the United Kingdom as well as articles from international journals. Like Westlaw IE, you can narrow your search of LexisLibrary to journals. You can then search for articles relevant to a particular topic or you can search for a specific article by searching for its name, author or citation.

(c) **HeinOnline (home.heinonline.org):** HeinOnline is a North American database and so while it is not useful for finding Irish legislation and case law, it is excellent for finding journal articles. It has a simple search function (as well as an advanced search function) and search results

---

[9] There are many reasons. Law departments tend to recommend journals subscriptions to their libraries that will be useful for their students, so by searching your institution's library, you are searching within a pool of journal subscriptions that are more likely to be useful to you. Moreover, if you are having trouble using the library's search functions, librarians will be on hand to help you out (support for other legal databases can be less helpful, personal and immediate).

will be returned with excerpts from each article, which makes it easier to determine whether an article might be useful for your research.

(d) JSTOR (www.jstor.org): Like HeinOnline, JSTOR is North American law centric. However, it includes a large selection of journal articles from a range of American and international journals. Many of JSTOR's articles are also open access. Like the other legal databases, it has both a simple search function and an advanced search function.

Sometimes, the subscription-based legal databases will not give you the results that you are looking for. In this situation, it is acceptable to go to a general search engine, to see if that will produce anything relevant. Google offers the Google Scholar search engine (**scholar. google.com**). Google Scholar can be a powerful tool for legal research – however, it is usually a double-edged sword. You must be aware of the limitations of Google Scholar whenever you use it. Google Scholar searches the entirety of the internet and then indexes the full text or metadata of scholarly literature – this means that if there is a freely available version of an article that matches your search criteria somewhere on the internet, Google Scholar should find it. The short links to the right of the titles of each result take you to a freely available version of that article. If there is no such short link, then clicking on the article title may take you to a freely accessible version of the article, but it may not. This can be useful if you have not been able to find anything helpful on the subscription-based legal databases.

However, since Google Scholar searches the whole of the internet, it will more than likely return many articles that are not at all relevant to your search terms, including non-law articles. This means that you may be faced with many irrelevant articles and you will have to spend more time picking through the results than you would if you performed the same search using a subscription-based legal database.

This is not to say that databases such as Westlaw IE or HeinOnline will never return irrelevant results to you – they will. Google Scholar is simply more likely to return irrelevant results because of the nature of where it searches for information. For this reason, you should start your journal article search on legal databases and then move to Google Scholar only if necessary. Google Scholar, like HeinOnline and JSTOR, is not a useful tool for finding Irish legislation or case law. It should be used for articles only.[10]

---

[10]   Google Scholar will also return results for relevant books, but unless the specific

3.2.5 Improving the likelihood of your searches returning relevant results

When you are searching for relevant sources on a topic, rather than searching for a specific source, there are a number of things you can do to make your search queries more effective. Using more keywords in your search can force the database to return more relevant results as you are giving it more information to work with. However, be careful that you do not overload the database with information – too many keywords may lead to the database not returning any results at all.

To make the most of legal databases, think not only about *what* you search for, but *how* you search. Consider using some of the following techniques to make your searches as relevant and useful as possible.

Search technique[11]	Explanation	Example
Connectors	Connectors (also referred to as Boolean operators[12]) define the relationship between your search terms. These connectors are **AND**, **OR** and **NOT**. <ul><li>Linking two words with **AND** will retrieve material containing both words.</li><li>Linking two words with **OR** will retrieve material containing either word (use this connector when searching for synonyms).</li><li>Linking two words with **NOT** will retrieve material containing the first, but not the second, word.</li></ul>	<ul><li>tort AND negligence AND sport</li><li>sport OR coaching</li><li>amateur NOT professional</li></ul>

---

information you want is available in an online preview of the book you will have to go back to your institution's library to see if they hold a physical or an electronic copy of that book, if it looks useful to you.

11 There will be slight differences between how these search techniques are used for each database. The 'help' (or equivalent) section of each database will usually confirm how each of these searches can be conducted on that database.

12 Boolean operators are named after the British mathematician George Boole, who developed the structures of algebraic logic upon which Boolean searching (and thus Boolean operators) are based. This is a method of electronic searching that is designed to help a database decide, when you give it a set of keywords, whether a particular item is relevant to your search by instructing it to only return results if they match your keywords *in a certain way*. For a deeper

Search technique[11]	Explanation	Example
Field searching	The advanced search function of most legal databases allows you to search specific fields (such as author, date, title). If you use these fields to search for specific words, then only material containing the words in the specified context will be retrieved.	Westlaw IE allows you to narrow your searches for cases to the following fields: Free Text; Party Names; Citation; Subject/Keyword.
Phrase searching	If you search for a phrase within a legal database, the material retrieved will typically include all of your search terms, but not necessarily in the same sentence or phrase. To limit your search to an exact phrase, surround the phrase with quotation marks (whether these are single or double depends on the database—check the 'help' section of the database to confirm).	"duty of care"
Truncation/ word expansion	A truncated word is one where the root of the word is included in the search, followed by a symbol (this is usually !, but it varies between databases—check the 'help' section of the database to confirm). A search using a truncated word will retrieve material containing words with the same root as the search term, but with various different word endings.	A search for **negligen!** on Westlaw IE retrieves material containing the following words: negligen**t**, negligen**ce**, negligen**tly**.
Wild card/ universal characters	Including a universal character (this is usually *, but it varies between databases—check the 'help' section of the database to confirm) in the middle of a word will retrieve material containing words with the same characters as the search term, but where the universal character acts as a placeholder and can be substituted for any other letter.	A search for **wom*n** on Westlaw IE retrieves material containing the following words: wom**a**n, wom**e**n.

discussion of Boolean operators, see Chapter 1 in: S Delaney, *Electronic Legal Research: An Integrated Approach* (2nd edn, Delmar Cengage Learning 2009).

Search technique[11]	Explanation	Example
Nearby words	If you want to search for material in which certain words are connected, but do not necessarily appear in a particular order, you can narrow your search results to those where two words appear within a particular number of words of each other. The character used for this varies between databases (check the 'help' section of the database to confirm) but is **/n** (where n is the number of words) on Westlaw IE.	A search for **sport /3 coaching** on Westlaw IE retrieves material where 'sport' and 'coaching' appear within three words of each other.
Searching within results	Once your search results are displayed, you can further narrow these down by searching for more specific search terms within the results—this will search only within the original results.	A search for "duty of care" on Westlaw IE can be further narrowed by searching for "minors" within the search results.

3.3 Effective reading

When you have found the sources that you are looking for, you will need to extract the information that you need from them. It should come as no surprise that legal research involves doing a lot of reading.[13] Many new law students are unprepared when they enter law school to undertake the kind of active, engaged reading of source material that is required to build a thorough understanding of the law and an ability to analyse and evaluate it rigorously.[14] Being able to read effectively and efficiently is a skill that every law student, lawyer and legal academic should aim to develop.

3.3.1 Key reading skills

This book does not claim to be an authority on reading skills – in fact, there are many academic pieces that have already provided excellent analysis of the skills involved in reading source material

---

[13] The importance of motivating yourself to do deep and detailed reading for your modules, and the problems caused by not doing so, is summarised well by Spencer and Seymour: Liesel Spencer and Elen Seymour, 'Reading Law: Motivating Digital Natives to "Do the Reading"' (2013) 23 Legal Education Review 177.

[14] For an excellent discussion of the reasons why, see: Patricia Grande Montana, 'Bridging the Reading Gap in the Law School Classroom' (2017) 45 Capital University Law Review 433.

effectively and efficiently.[15] Rather, this section aims to distil the research already conducted on reading skills into a shorter and more manageable summary.

Someone who is an effective and efficient reader will do the following things when conducting their detailed research:

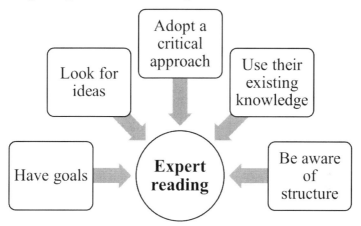

(1) **Have goals for your reading:** You should always read with a goal.[16] To establish your particular reading goal or goals, approach your reading with a clear purpose – ask yourself:

- *what* you want to get out of reading a particular source;
- *why* you have selected a particular source to read; and
- *whether* you think that the source in front of you is likely to give you what you need.

Always keep your goals in mind as you read – move on to a different source if the one you are reading is not meeting your reading goal. Keep reading if the source is meeting your goals, even if much of what you are reading feels familiar. For example, you might already know the law discussed in

---

[15] See Ruth McKinney, *Reading Like a Lawyer: Time-Saving Strategies for Reading Law Like an Expert* (Carolina Academic Press 2014); Julian Hermida, 'The Importance of Teaching Academic Reading Skills in First-Year University Courses' (2009) 3 International Journal of Research and Review 20; Alex Steel *et al.*, 'Critical Legal Reading: The Elements, Strategies and Dispositions Needed to Master this Essential Skill' (2016) 26(1) Legal Education Review 187; Peter Dewitz, 'Reading Law – Three Suggestions for Legal Education (1995) 27 University of Toledo Law Review 657.

[16] The purpose of your reading is crucial to both your reading efficiency and your ultimate understanding of the text. People can, and have, written entire PhDs on this fact: Regina Calloway, 'Why do You Read? Toward a More Comprehensive Model of Reading Comprehension: The Role of Standards of Coherence, Reading Goals, and Interest (Doctoral Thesis, University of Pittsburgh 2019).

a journal article, but if your goal is to understand or critique the perspectives of various authors on that law (rather than to learn what the law says), then you need to keep reading the article.

(2) **Look for the main ideas in what you have read:** You should actively look for the main ideas, arguments or principles of law contained within the text, rather than just passively take in the text in front of your eyes. You do not necessarily have to read every word of the source in order to do this. Constantly ask yourself whether you understand the main argument or legal principle behind the source as a whole, as well as just understanding what is written in each paragraph.

Once you have reached the end of the source, try to summarise for yourself what the main message was. Once you have done this, reflect on that message – was it what you thought it was going to be as you were reading the text? Did you understand it? Do you need to read the source again, or do you need to read another source to confirm or clarify your understanding of the message?

(3) **Adopt a critical approach to your reading:** Being critical in an academic context does not mean being negative. It means not taking what you read at face value.

Taylor and colleagues summarise critical reading in the following way:

> critical reading involves interaction with the text... knowledge can be challenged, evaluated, accepted and rejected by the reader. This process of questioning, filtering and selecting information will have a transforming effect which typifies learning ... there should be some evidence of learning which resulted in changed conceptions by having learners manifest as creatively as possible some qualitative shift in understanding, insight, or perspective as a result of reading.[17]

Achieving this means asking yourself certain practical questions while you are reading:

- is the text based on any assumptions that you disagree or agree with?;
- is the opinion put forward by the author something that you share or do not share?; and

---

[17] Lyndal Taylor and others, 'Reading Is Critical' (2001) 3 University of Technology Sydney Law Review 126.

- in what context was the text written, what is the author's motivation and do these things explain the arguments and opinions put forward by the author?

Do not simply accept what a source says. Think about whether you agree with it and why, and what new understanding of the law you have gained following your reading of the source.

(4) Read in light of what you already know about the topic: Read passages in more or less depth depending on your goals and on what you already understand. For example, if you are not reading in order to critique and are just reading for knowledge, you can skip over bits of the text that discuss law that you already understand. Read in light of what you do not already know about the topic.[18] Check what technical terms or ideas mean as you read, if needed. There is no shame in doing this, and indeed, it is the smart, scholarly thing to do. The whole point of scholarship is to learn things that we do not already know. If you are reading a source without understanding what the key terms within it mean, then you will not learn very much at all.

(5) Read with an awareness of how the structure of the source can help you achieve you reading goals: Be familiar with what is where in the source, before you start reading. Apply what you know about the structure of similar pieces to the current piece. For example, court cases generally contain a summary of the facts first, before the judge lays out his or her judgment. If you already know the basic facts, and only need to read the judge's analysis and conclusion on the legal principles that apply to them, then you know to scroll past the facts and look for the heading that indicates where the judgment itself begins.[19]

---

[18] The process of thinking about what you do and do not know is called metacognition. As Bloom Grisé puts it, '[i]t is essential to develop an awareness of when you understand something and when you do not. This is so important that major law firms have stated that a key skill new lawyers need to master is to "know when they don't know." Studies have shown that we often overestimate our comprehension. Therefore, if you think you might not understand something, assume that you need to go back over the material': Jane Bloom Grisé, *Critical Reading for Success in Law School and Beyond* (West Academic Publishing 2017) 14.

[19] The structure of judgments is also the example used by Christensen, who adds that 'comprehension proceeds more smoothly if the reader understands the organizational structure of the text … A new reader could easily become confused by [a judgment's] unusual structure': Leah M Christensen, 'Legal Reading and Success in Law School: An Empirical Study' (2007) 30 Seattle University Law Review 603, 607.

3.3.2 Note-taking while reading

Effective and efficient reading does not just involve the physical act of reading the words on the page. It also involves taking notes while you read. You may think that taking notes would slow down your research, but the opposite is true. Note-taking is an indispensable part of academic reading.

(1) **Taking notes makes it easier to engage with the text that you are reading:** Concentrating on writing down what you have learned, what you do or do not understand, what you agree or disagree with, makes it much easier for you to actually do those things. If you rely on simply thinking about these things you can easily slip into a mode of passively absorbing information without engaging with that information. Physical note-taking forces you to perform the mental processes that you need to perform in order to properly engage with what you are reading.

(2) **Taking notes makes it easier to read critically:** You can look at what you have just written about the text and use that to give your full attention to reflecting or questioning further, without having to hold the initial thoughts you had in your head at the same time.

(3) **Taking notes makes it easier to monitor your research:** If you have a record of what you have achieved with your reading, you are less likely to forget what you have learned, or what stage of your research you have got to. You have a physical record of whether your reading has been meeting your goals or not. This record makes it easier to identify what you still have left to read in order to meet your goals and to plan out how to do this.

(4) **Taking notes makes it easier to understand what you are reading:** You truly understand something when you can explain it clearly and accurately to others, and the first step of achieving this is being able to explain it clearly and accurately to yourself. Taking notes is a way of manifesting your understanding of what you have read for yourself. You then have a record that you can come back to. This will help you to determine whether you understood a particular legal concept or principle as well as you thought you did when you were reading. It will also help you to see what you understood a source to mean. A written record will allow you to check or reinforce your understanding.

Note taking is a personal process – find a method that works well for you. This could be annotating original or electronic copies of sources, keeping notes in a journal or an electronic document, drawing diagrams, or something different. Whatever method you pick, just make sure that it is easy to organise, easy to navigate and easy to read. There is no point in making notes in an illegible scrawl or some arcane concoction of abbreviations and symbols for which you cannot remember the meaning later on.

3.4 Chapter summary

- Consider the full range of sources available to you during your research – do not just read textbooks.

- Distinguish between primary and secondary sources – for statements of what the law is, always refer to the primary sources.

- There will usually be a host of legal databases available to you. When you start your research consider which databases to use and be prepared to use multiple databases during the course of your research.

- Legal research, particularly online, is not just about what you are researching, but how you conduct that research – dedicate time to searching databases thoroughly and correctly to get the most out of them.

- Make notes as you research – this will help you to read actively, rather than passively.

Part II

The Writing Process

Chapter 4

Effective (Legal) Writing
– the Building Blocks

Part I of this book considered how to conduct legal research. Preparation and thorough research for a piece of legal writing – whether it is an essay, an email to a client or a presentation – is an essential step in the legal writing process.

In writing, particularly legal writing, it can be easy to get caught up in making sure that what you write is correct. Because of this, you may spend most of your time focused on the substance of a piece of legal writing without giving much thought to its style. Yet effective legal writing is about both substance and style.

Of course, you want your reader to focus on what you are saying in a piece of legal writing. But for this to happen, your reader must not be distracted by stylistic mistakes or peculiarities. Poorly written sentences, spelling and grammatical errors, and unwieldy paragraphs distract and even detract from the substance of your writing. If you were to read a textbook or a newspaper article that was full of errors and which looked hastily thrown together, you may worry that an author who gave so little consideration to the presentation of his or her work may also have been careless as to the work's accuracy. Do not underestimate the negative impression that poor writing can leave with the reader. A primary goal of effective legal writing is, therefore, to remove stylistic distractions so that your reader can focus on the substance that you have done so much research for.

> **Practical Tip:**
>
> Good writing should go unnoticed by the reader. Bad writing will not. If you spend time working on your legal writing, do not get disheartened if you do not receive positive feedback on it. This hopefully means that the reader has been able to focus on what you have written and is able to engage with the substance of your work without distraction.

The writing skills discussed in this book are not just important at third level. They will remain relevant when you begin applying for jobs and once you start your professional life.

- Graduate employers will expect you to have good written communication skills and will be assessing these from the moment they look at your application or CV.
- If you go on to work as a solicitor, much of your communication with your colleagues, clients and solicitors in other law firms will be in writing. You will be expected to write precisely, accurately and professionally. This is not just people being pedantic, it is a matter of professional necessity – a misplaced comma or a confusingly defined concept could change the meaning of a sentence. When this impacts on your client's rights or obligations, the implications can be significant.[1]
- While barristers may be engaged for their skills as orators, much of their advice and other interactions, including with the court, are in writing. The ability to convey and explain complex legal arguments in writing is, therefore, fundamental.

Part II of this book focuses on the writing process in the context of legal writing. Chapter 4 discusses basic aspects of all good writing – spelling, grammar, punctuation. Chapter 5 considers appropriate writing style, impactful sentences and proofreading. While these two chapters are tailored to discuss these various aspects in the context of legal writing, many of the principles and conventions covered are relevant to any situation where good written communication is called for. Chapter 6 discusses citations, referencing and the importance of avoiding plagiarism.

---

[1] In *Ned Murphy v Paddy McKeown and Adelaide McCarthy* [2020] IECA 75, for example, a significant amount of time before the court was taken up with arguments as to whether a missing comma in a bank's name in a document drafted by solicitors was inadvertent or deliberate and whether the absence of the comma changed the legal entity named in the document.

Practical Tip:

Use your essays and other assessments as an opportunity not just to build your legal knowledge, but to improve your written communication generally. No matter how good your ideas or research skills are, if your lecturer cannot work out what you are trying to say in an essay or if he or she gets the impression that you cannot be bothered to spend time on the formality of your work, your grade may suffer. Take the time now to think about how to clearly convey your ideas, pay attention to your spelling and grammar, and build in time to proofread your work. These are skills that you will get better at over time and which you will need to possess when you enter professional life.

4.1 Spelling

4.1.1 Spelling: take particular care to get this right

With spellchecking functions now available on all word processing software, there should be no spelling mistakes in your legal writing. Spelling mistakes suggest that you have not adequately proofread your work and may give the impression of a lack of care. Make sure, therefore, that the spellcheck on your computer is turned on and the default proofing language is set to English (Ireland) or English (United Kingdom) – be wary of this proofing language being set to English (United States) unless the American spelling of words is relevant in the context.

Your computer's spellcheck should ensure that you avoid obvious spelling errors in your legal writing. However, what spellcheck will not necessarily pick up is where you spell the names of parties, judges or sometimes places incorrectly, or where you misspell a word, but that misspelling happens to be a correct spelling of a different word (for example: 'Hugh Court' rather than 'High Court'). Pay attention to any proper nouns used in your legal writing, check each of these individually when you are proofreading your work – there are many company law lecturers that have read (and despaired at) essays that refer to the case of *Salmon v A Salmon & Co Ltd* when they should be referring to *Salomon v A Salomon & Co Ltd*.[2]

---

[2] [1896] UKHL 1, [1897] AC 22.

> **Practical Tip:**
>
> If you do most of your legal writing on one computer (for example, your laptop), it might be worth adding proper nouns that you commonly use to your computer's custom dictionary. This will stop your computer autocorrecting proper nouns with which it is not familiar.

> **Practical Tip:**
>
> Double (or triple) check that you have spelt people's names correctly when you email them and that you have spelt law firms' names correctly in your applications. These are very simple things to get right, but they will stand out prominently if you get them wrong.

4.1.2 Spelling: common spelling mix-ups

In addition to avoiding obvious spelling mistakes and ensuring that you spell proper nouns correctly, be conscious about how you spell words that are frequently confused. These are words that sound alike and the spelling of both is correct, but they are distinct words that can change the meaning of a sentence.

If you find that you mix up words that sound alike, you may find it helpful to have a list of such words. Refer to this list as you proofread to remind you which words you should pay particular attention to. Set out below is a list of commonly mixed up words.

Advice/Advise	• 'Advice' (noun) means a recommendation or opinion. • 'Advise' (verb) means to offer a recommendation or opinion.
Affect/Effect	• 'Affect' (typically a verb) means to influence or make a difference to something. • 'Effect' (typically a noun) means a result. • 'Effect' (can also be used as a verb) means to bring about.
Council/Counsel	• 'Council' (noun) means a meeting or grouping. • 'Counsel' (verb) means to offer advice. • 'Counsel' (noun) means someone offering advice.
Discreet/Discrete	• 'Discreet' (adjective) means careful or sensitive. • 'Discrete' (adjective) means separate or individual.

Its/It's	• 'Its' is the possessive of 'it' and is an exception to the apostrophe rule referred to below. • 'It's' is a contraction of 'it is' or 'it has' and should be avoided.
Judgment/Judgement	• 'Judgment' means a pronouncement of a judge. • 'Judgement' means someone's opinion.
Licence/License	• 'Licence' (noun) means a permit to own or do something. • 'License' (verb) means the act of granting someone a licence.
Practice/Practise	• 'Practice' (noun) is used in the context of a lawyer's practice. • 'Practise' (verb) is used in the context of 'to practise something'.
Principal/Principle	• 'Principal' means main or most important. • 'Principle' means rule, idea, or belief.
Their/There/They're	• 'Their' is the possessive of 'they'. • 'There' indicates direction or position. It is also used to introduce a noun or clause. • 'They're' is a contraction of 'they are' and should be avoided.
To/Too	• 'To' is a preposition used to express motion, direction or a change. • 'Too' is an adverb signifying excess or addition.

4.2 Grammar and punctuation

As well as checking your spelling, most word processing software will also try to check the correctness of your grammar and punctuation. However, the rules of grammar and punctuation are more nuanced than those of spelling. You must, therefore, be vigilant when checking your grammar and punctuation.

4.2.1 Grammar: the basics

Before discussing aspects of grammatical sentences, ensure that you are familiar with the various components of a sentence.

Component	Definition	Used in a sentence
Noun	A noun is a word used to name a person, place, thing or idea.	The *hand grenade* hit the *display stand* as the *child* and *woman* ran towards the *door*.
Proper Noun	Proper nouns are nouns used to identify specific people, places, or organisations. Proper nouns should always start with capital letters.	The *Supreme Court* heard the case on the first *Wednesday* in *September*. *MacMenamin J* delivered the judgment.

Component	Definition	Used in a sentence
Pronoun	A pronoun is a word that replaces a noun: she, he, we, it, they or them.	Emily and Caden arrived in court. *They* ignored each other at the entrance.
Adjective	An adjective is a word that describes an attribute of a noun.	The *damaged* trophies shattered and spun across the *empty* floor.
Verb	A verb is a word that describes an action, a state or an occurrence.	Emily *explained* the situation to the policewoman. The policewoman *noted* this in her notebook while *hiding* her scepticism.
Adverb	An adverb is a word that describes or modifies a verb, adjective, adverb or phrase. Adverbs usually end with '–ly'.	Emily *quickly* recovered her composure. Caden started crying *loudly*.
Preposition	A preposition is a word that connects a noun or pronoun to the verb in a sentence, such as 'in', 'on', 'to', 'with', 'over', 'when', 'off'. It usually explains the relationship between the noun/pronoun and the verb in terms of direction, location or time.	The glass from the trophies spread *over* the floor. The glass was still there *when* the police arrived.
Conjunction	A conjunction is a word that connects two parts of a sentence together, such as 'and', 'but', 'for', 'nor', 'yet', 'or', 'so', 'because'.	The sports complex is large, *but* the shouting can be heard clearly through the speaker system.

4.2.2 Grammar: write in complete sentences

Try to write in complete sentences. Sentences that are grammatically complete and correct are easier to understand than sentences that use poor or complicated grammar.

A simple sentence will usually consist of a subject and a verb. It may also consist of an object. For example: 'The armed man [*subject*] ran [*verb*] past [the security woman [*object*]]'. As discussed below in Section 5.3.5, writing in the passive voice can allow you to avoid stating the actor in a sentence. However, you should be aiming to write in the active voice as much as possible and when doing so, you should ensure that your sentences are complete. Remember, when writing a sentence always ask yourself 'who/what did what to whom?'.

When a sentence expresses a complete thought and contains a subject and a verb, it is an independent clause.

- Simple sentences contain one independent clause (for example: 'The armed man threw the grenade').
- Complex sentences contain an independent clause and a subordinate clause (for example: 'Emily rushed towards the exit [*independent clause*], even though the armed man was still shouting [*subordinate clause*]').
- Compound sentences contain multiple independent clauses (for example: 'She ran quietly towards the exit [*independent clause*], but she failed to consider the reaction of Caden [*independent clause*]').

A mixture of simple, complex and compound sentences can make your legal writing more interesting.

4.2.3 Grammar: common grammar mistakes

The rules of grammar are slightly more flexible than those applying to spelling – for example, a reader is likely to be more forgiving if you end your sentence with a preposition than if you spell his or her name incorrectly. Nevertheless, there are a number of common grammar mistakes that you should try to avoid.

(1) **Using run-on sentences**: A run-on sentence occurs when two or more independent clauses are connected improperly. This could be the case if:

- the clauses are separated only by a comma and no conjunction (and, but, for, nor, yet, or, so) is used to connect them (for example: 'The grenade explodes, shrapnel goes flying.' This sentence is missing 'and' after the comma to connect the clauses); or
- the clauses need to be separated by a full stop or semi-colon (for example: 'Caden and Emily run for the exit, Caden kicks over the display'. Separate these two clauses with a full stop).

In any sentence in which you use a comma, check whether it is a run-on sentence.

(2) **Not ensuring subject-verb agreement and pronoun-antecedent agreement**: Make sure that within a sentence: (a) the verb agrees in number with the subject; and (b) the pronoun agrees in number and gender with the word that a pronoun refers back to (known as the antecedent).

- If the subject is singular, the verb must be singular, if the subject is plural, the verb must be plural. Be vigilant when the subject of a sentence is a collective noun (for example: 'the group of students', 'a collection of pens'). Collective nouns are frequently followed by a singular verb when you are referring to one collective thing, although this will depend on context (for example: 'a group of students is waiting outside' takes a singular verb since there is only one group of students and those students are acting as a unit).
- If the antecedent is singular and female, the pronoun must be singular and female, if the antecedent is plural and male, the pronoun must be plural and male (and vice versa).

Example:

Subject-verb agreement
- **Incorrect:** 'As a result of his injuries, *Caden have* ongoing medical needs.'
- **Correct:** 'As a result of his injuries, *Caden has* ongoing medical needs.'

- **Incorrect:** 'The *box* of cables *are* priced at €4.'
- **Correct:** 'The *box* of cables *is* priced at €4.'

Pronoun-antecedent agreement
- **Incorrect:** '*Emily* fails to look over *their* shoulder.'
- **Correct:** '*Emily* fails to look over *her* shoulder' as 'Emily' is female and singular.

---

(3) **Mixing up 'I' and 'me':** The pronouns 'I' and 'me' are frequently mixed up. Use 'I' when you are the subject of a sentence (for example: 'I attended the basketball game') and 'me' when you are the object (for example: 'the basketball bounced and hit me').

> **Practical Tip:**
>
> Difficulty can arise when there are multiple parties referred to in a sentence (for example: which is correct: 'the basketball bounced and hit my friend and I' or 'the basketball bounced and hit my friend and me'?). The rule above continues to apply – 'I' when you are the subject; 'me' when you are the object. As a result, 'the basketball bounced and hit my friend and me' is correct.
>
> The easiest way to get this right is to imagine that the other party is not referred to in the sentence and then to read the sentence to yourself – your ear should pick up whether you are using 'I' or 'me' correctly. For example, it is easy to conclude that 'the basketball bounced and hit I' is incorrect. You can then just add the other party back into the sentence.

(4) **Using contractions**: A contraction is where two words are shortened to form a single word divided by an apostrophe. Commonly used contractions are: 'it's' (a contraction of 'it is' or 'it has' *not* the possessive form of 'it'), 'you're' (a contraction of 'you are'), 'haven't' (a contraction of 'have not').

Contractions have no place in legal writing, and you should never use them.

> **Practical Tip:**
>
> The 'it's' (contraction), 'its' (possessive) distinction trips up many people. Pay attention to this in your legal writing. If you find you mix up these words frequently, do a word search for 'it's' in your final draft document. Then change any 'it's' to 'it is', 'it has' or 'its' as appropriate.

(5) **Incorrectly or inconsistently using ampersand (&)**: An ampersand is a symbol representing 'and'. In legal writing you should not use an ampersand in place of 'and' in a sentence. Its only use is when '&' forms part of a proper noun (for example: Mason Hayes & Curran LLP).

(6) **'Should of', 'could of', 'would of'**: 'Should of', 'could of', 'would of' are grammatically incorrect and you should never use them. Nevertheless, you often see these phrases written when referring to an opportunity that was missed or something that did not happen. The correct phrases to use in this context (and the correct expansions of the contractions 'should've', 'could've' and 'would've') are 'should *have*', 'could *have*' and 'would *have*'.

> **Example:**
> - **Correct:** 'I should *have* called you earlier.'
> - **Incorrect:** 'I should *of* called you earlier.'

4.2.4 Punctuation

Punctuation helps the reader to understand your writing by adding in pauses, stops, intonation, emphasis and connections that come naturally when sentences are spoken, but which are otherwise absent from written words.

Perhaps even more so than spelling and grammar, you may assume that correct use of punctuation is so basic that you do not need to give it much active thought. However, using punctuation correctly is surprisingly difficult and requires you to consider not just what you are writing, but *how* you want it to be read.[3]

(1) **Full Stops (.):** Use full stops to manage sentence length. If a long sentence can more easily be read as two shorter sentences, use a full stop to divide it in two.

  If you are including a footnote at the end of a sentence, the footnote mark should be included *after* the full stop. Each footnote should itself end with a full stop.

  If you are using a full stop in the middle of a sentence, for example as part of an abbreviated word or in a company name, make sure that the word following the full stop is not accidentally capitalised.

(2) **Commas (,):** Commas are useful tools for making your legal writing more readable. They are also commonly used incorrectly. Be mindful that too many commas in a sentence can make it hard to follow. If you have a sentence that includes numerous commas, consider whether it should be broken down into separate sentences.

  Commas can be used in a number of situations.
  (a) **To separate text that could otherwise be included**

---

[3] Punctuation is also relevant in terms of statutory interpretation, see statement of McDonald J in *Re Finnegan (a debtor)* [2019] IEHC 66, [64], 'In my view, this submission by counsel for the practitioner has considerable force. It is borne out by a consideration of the punctuation within section 115A(2). In this context, notwithstanding the approach which has traditionally been taken in England &Wales, the Irish Courts have regard to punctuation as an aid to statutory interpretation. This is clear, for example, from the judgment of Hardiman J. in *Minister for Justice v. Bailey* [2012] 4 I.R. 1 at page 72. It is also apparent from the judgment of Fennelly J. in *Twil Ltd v. Kearney* [2001] 4 I.R. 476 at page 492.'

in parentheses. If using commas for this purpose, include two commas, one immediately before and one immediately after the text that you want to separate.

Example:
Using parentheses: 'After the basketball game, Emily (who is the team's coach) got into the bus …' **Using commas:** 'After the basketball game, Emily, who is the team's coach, got into the bus …'

(b) For clarity, where the meaning of the sentence would be unclear without the commas.

Example:
'Caden was not killed, mercifully.' Without this comma, the sentence 'Caden was not killed mercifully' means something very different.

(c) Before certain conjunctions ('and', 'but', 'for', 'nor', 'yet', 'or', 'so') to separate two independent clauses. Be careful when using commas in this way – it can encourage very long sentences that would work better as two separate sentences.

(d) To separate items in a series of three or more items. Commas are used to separate three or more words or phrases in a list. Whether a comma should appear after the penultimate item in the list and before the conjunction (known as the 'Oxford' or 'serial' comma) remains debated.

Example:
Simple comma: Emily, Caden and James entered the court at the same time. **Serial/Oxford comma:** Emily, Caden, and James entered the court at the same time.

Use of the serial/Oxford comma is usually a matter of personal preference although if you are preparing a piece of legal writing for your employer or a publisher, check to make sure that they do not have a policy on this in place. The serial/Oxford comma can also be helpful in removing ambiguity as to whether the final two items in the list are separate items or should be viewed as a single item.

> **Example:**
>
> In the sentence 'Emily arrived in court with her two barristers, Josh Sidwell and Hermione Form' it is not clear whether Emily arrived in the court with four people – her two barristers, plus Josh and Hermione or if she arrived in court with two people, her barristers who are called Josh and Hermione. In this context a serial/Oxford comma would bring clarity where Josh and Hermione are separate items in the list (and so are not Emily's barristers).

(e) **To separate a number of adjectives that describe the same noun.** As a general rule, if you can reverse the order of the adjectives without changing the meaning of the sentence, then use a comma to separate them. If you cannot reverse the order, do not use a comma.

> **Example:**
>
> **Comma needed:** 'The grenade was *expensive, powerful* but poorly maintained' (since you can reverse the order of expensive and powerful without changing the meaning of the sentence).
>
> **No comma needed:** 'The *vibrant red* car arrived' (since you would not reverse the order of vibrant and red).

(f) **Before a quotation** included within a sentence.

> **Example:**
>
> The man with the hand grenade said, 'I do not want to hurt anyone, but if anyone moves, I will do it'.

(g) **To separate introductory or contrasting elements in a sentence.**

> **Example:**
>
> **Separating introductory elements:** 'While she had done everything she was supposed to do, Emily was still worried about what had happened.'
>
> **Separating contrasting elements:** 'Emily was a hard worker, but she lacked attention to detail.'

(3) **Colons (:) and semi-colons (;)**: Colons introduce a pause between related information. In this way, colons can be used to introduce:

- a list of items (items in a list should be separated by semi-colons);
- a quotation, particularly a lengthy quotation introduced by a complete sentence (in place of a comma); or
- an elaboration or explanation of an earlier statement. When a colon is used to introduce an elaboration or explanation, the words before the colon should form a complete sentence. The words after the colon do not need to form a complete sentence.

Do not follow a colon with a capital letter (unless referring to a proper noun).

> **Example:**
>
> **Introducing a list:** 'In her statement to the police, Emily noted the following: (1) she had reacted quickly to a stressful situation; (2) ...'
>
> **Introducing an elaboration/explanation:** 'There are three elements to indicate whether a duty of care arises in a particular situation: proximity of the parties; foreseeable of the damage; and the absence of a compelling reason not to impose one.'

Like colons, semi-colons introduce a pause between related information. Semi-colons can be used to:

- separate items in a list (but never to introduce a list); or
- separate two related clauses where each clause could be read as an independent sentence.

While you should not overuse semi-colons in your legal writing, they can be useful if you want to vary your sentence length. Do not follow a semi-colon with a capital letter (unless referring to a proper noun).

> **Example:**
>
> 'Emily was a diligent coach; she hoped to one day coach a professional team.'

(4) **Apostrophes (')**: In legal writing, apostrophes should only be used to indicate possession.

If the subject is singular, the apostrophe is placed before the 's'.

> **Example:**
>
> 'Caden's injury...'

If the subject is plural, the apostrophe is placed after the 's'.

> **Example:**
>
> 'The parties' disagreement as to the order of events ...'

If the subject is singular but ends in an 's', the apostrophe is usually placed after the 's' (although it is also correct to include a second 's' after the apostrophe).

> **Example:**
>
> Both 'The Cispheil Nets' away game' and 'The Cispheil Nets's away game' are correct.

Apostrophes should never be used to indicate that something is plural. They should also never be used to form a contraction (see Section 4.2.3 above). Remember, 'it's' is not the possessive of 'it', it is a contraction of 'it is' or 'it has'. The possessive of 'it' is 'its'.

> **Practical Tip:**
>
> Do not make the mistake of adding an apostrophe when you are referring to decades in a numerical format. The correct format is 'in the 1980s ...' not 'in the 1980's'.

(5) **Other punctuation**:
  - **Exclamation marks (!):** In legal writing, limit your use of more informal punctuation, such as exclamation marks. You should not, for example, use exclamation marks to show surprise or shock. The only situation in which you are likely to use an exclamation mark in legal writing is if you are quoting a statement that includes one.
  - **Question marks (?):** Questions expressed as interrogatives that end with a question mark are also generally not appropriate (for example: 'Surely that cannot be right?').
  - **Dashes (–):** Dashes can be used to set information apart. They create emphasis and identify the added information

as important.[4] When using dashes in this way, you will generally need to include two dashes; one on either side of the separated information.

Example:

'The judge – who had long been concerned about the growing level of noise in the courts – issued a warning to the parties.'

Dashes are also used to indicate date range (in place of 'and'). For example: '1990–2000'.

- **Hyphens (-):** Hyphens do not introduce a pause (and note they are physically shorter than dashes). They are used between two or more words that together modify a subsequent word in the sentence. For example: 'it was an *open-ended* question'.

  Hyphens can also be used to connect some prefixes and suffixes to words – use a hyphen when:
    o a prefix is followed by a proper noun. For example: 'mid-September';
    o one of the following prefixes precedes a word: 'all-', 'ex-' (in the sense of past – for example: 'ex-wife') or 'self-'; or
    o certain suffixes follow a word: '-type', '-elect', or '-designate'.

- **Ellipses (...):** An ellipsis signals that one or more words are missing from a quotation. Ellipses can be very useful if you want to include a quotation in your legal writing, but not all words in the quotation are relevant.

---

[4] There are two kinds of dashes, en-dashes (–) and slightly longer em-dashes (—). The longer em-dash is more commonly used in the United States, but it is always worth checking whether your employer or institution has a preference as to which dashes you use and when.

> **Example:**
>
> 'The defendant is entitled to assume also that by now it is common knowledge, and the experience of everybody who uses a bus, that because of their sheer size and the volumes of traffic in which they typically travel in the city they tend to sway and lurch a bit, even when driven with great care.'[5]
>
> This could be written as:
>
> '... it is common knowledge and the experience of everybody who uses a bus, that ... they tend to sway and lurch a bit...'[6]

When using ellipses, ensure that you do not remove so much from a quoted passage as to change its meaning. Particularly in academic legal writing you sometimes see quoted passages that have had crucial words removed and replaced with ellipses so that their meaning changes completely. This is unprofessional and lacks integrity.

- **Square brackets ([ ]):** You will find square brackets used quite frequently in academic legal writing. Use square brackets when you are altering a quotation. This would be the case if you are adding words or letters to a quotation or removing letters from the quotation to ensure it is clear or to make it work within the structure of your sentence. If you are removing whole words from a quotation you should use ellipses rather than square brackets.

> **Example:**
>
> **Original quotation:** 'The standard of reasonable care is that which is to be demanded in the circumstances.'[7]
>
> **To make it work within your sentence:** 'As noted by Asquith LJ in *Daborn v Bath Tramways Motor Co Ltd & T Rogersey*,[8] "[t]he standard of reasonable care is that which is to be demanded in the circumstances."'

In academic legal writing, some styles of legal citation use square brackets in footnotes when a pinpoint reference is to a paragraph number as distinct from a page number.

---

5   *McGarr v Dublin Bus/Bus Átha Cliath* [2016] IECA 366 [33].
6   *ibid.*
7   *Daborn v Bath Tramways Motor Co & T Rogersey* [1946] 2 All ER 333.
8   *ibid.*

Outside of academic legal writing, square brackets are used by legal practitioners to indicate that something is to be confirmed, checked or added in a document before that document can be said to be in final form.

> **Example:**
>
> 'The parties agree that a fee of [€4,000] will be paid to X and a fee of [€5,000] will be paid to Y. [*amounts to be confirmed*]'

When you are dealing with a document that has been through various drafts, always do a final word search for '[' and ']' before finalising it to make sure there is no information outstanding.

4.3 Capital letters, defined terms and acronyms

4.3.1 Capital letters

Incorrect use of capital letters is a frequent error made in legal writing.

Other than at the start of sentences, there are a few situations where capital letters are relevant.

1. The first letter of proper nouns (such as the name of a person, place, a particular court, or organisation) should be capitalised.

> **Example:**
>
> - A person's name: 'Emily Holloway', 'Ms Holloway', 'Emily', '*McComiskey v McDermott*'.[9]
> - The name of a place: 'Dublin', 'the United States of America'.
> - The name of courts: 'the District Court', 'the Circuit Court', 'the High Court', 'the Court of Appeal', 'the Supreme Court'. This also applies to courts in other jurisdictions, for example: 'the Supreme Court of the United Kingdom'. If you are just referring to the courts generally, do not capitalise the first letter.
> - The name of an organisation: 'Maynooth University', 'Transparency Ireland', 'Fountain Court Chambers'.
> - The title of legislative or similar instruments: 'the Companies Act 2014', 'the National Minimum Wage Order 2020'.

Students frequently use capitalisation in proper nouns inconsistently – for example, they might write 'Supreme Court' as 'Supreme court'. When proofreading your legal

---

[9]   *McComiskey v McDermott* [1974] IR 75.

writing, do a word search for any proper nouns used and ensure these are correctly and consistently capitalised.

2.   Words or phrases that you have defined or written as acronyms in your legal writing (for example, the 'Agreement' or the 'EU') should also be consistently capitalised (see Sections 4.3.2 and 4.3.3 below). If you capitalise a word that is not a proper noun, ensure that you have previously defined it in your document (or that you have referred to a document where it is defined).

Other than at the start of a sentence, for proper nouns, in defined terms or acronyms, your legal writing should not include capital letters. Including random capital letters in the middle of a sentence could confuse the reader and lead them to believe that a word is a defined term. It could also give the reader the impression that you have copied and pasted a phrase from another source without modifying it to fit within your sentence (and without adequately referencing that other source).

4.3.2 Defined terms

A defined term is a word or phrase that has been given a specific meaning in a document beyond its everyday meaning. That word or phrase will keep the meaning given to it each time it is used in the document. In legal writing, defined terms can be used to bring greater clarity to a document and reduce the risk of a reader getting confused by inconsistent terminology (see Section 5.3.8 below for a discussion of the importance of consistency in legal writing). Defined terms can also be helpful in managing a document's word count as once a definition is provided, it does not need to be repeated.

> **Example:**
>
> 'In an appeal on 14 December 2020 against the decision of Ryan J in the High Court (the 'Appeal'), Ms Holloway argued that Ryan J erred in law in holding that she could be held liable for the actions of the armed man in the sports complex. During the Appeal, Ms Holloway made the following arguments...'
>
> Explanation: Because the 'Appeal' is defined in the first sentence, it does not need to be defined again in the second sentence. Every subsequent reference in the document to the word 'Appeal' will mean the appeal on 14 December 2020 against the decision of Ryan J in the High Court.

The first letter of each word in a defined term is usually capitalised (even though a defined term is not a proper noun). This helps the reader to identify defined terms and signals to the reader that they must find where that term is defined in order to understand its specific meaning.

Where you include the definitions of your defined terms will depend on the length of your document, personal preference and/ or your institution or employer's requirements. For shorter legal documents and academic articles, definitions can be built into the body of the document between parentheses (these are known as 'running' definitions).

> **Example:**
>
> 'In Ireland, the law on concurrent wrongdoers is covered by s 11(1) of the Civil Liability Act 1961 (the '1961 Act'), which defines concurrent wrongdoers as...'

For longer documents, a list of definitions might instead be included at the start of the document in an interpretation or definitions section or in a schedule at the back of the document. If you include a list of definitions either in an interpretation section or in a schedule, make sure that these are in alphabetical order.

> **Example:**
>
> 'Agreement' means agreement dated 14 December 2020 between X and Y.
> 'Cover Letter' means ...
> 'Duty of Care' means ...

How you choose to highlight where a term is defined is a matter of personal and/or employer preference. Academic publishers or your lecturers may also express a preferred approach to definitions, which you should consult if relevant. Some people choose to make the defined term bold when it appears with its definition, some put the term in single or double quotation marks, some people do both. Whatever approach you use, make sure you use it consistently. Once a term is defined, you do not need to continue to make it bold or to surround it with quotation marks in the rest of the document. Just make sure you continue to consistently capitalise the first letter of the term.

> **Example:**
>
> **Quotation marks:** 'In an appeal on 14 December 2020 against the decision of Ryan J in the High Court (the 'Appeal'), Ms Holloway argued that Ryan J erred in law in holding that she could be held liable for the actions of the armed man in the sports complex. During the Appeal, Ms Holloway made the following arguments...'
>
> **Bold:** 'In an appeal on 14 December 2020 against the decision of Ryan J in the High Court (the **Appeal**), Ms Holloway argued that Ryan J erred in law in holding that she could be held liable for the actions of the armed man in the sports complex. During the Appeal, Ms Holloway made the following arguments...'

Though defined terms can be very useful in legal writing, do use them with care.

- Do not define something that you do not refer to again in the document – a defined term is only useful if you will be using the term more than once in a document.
- Always be consistent in the terminology you use – once a term is defined, you must use that exact terminology every time you refer to the same thing in your document.
- Do not overuse defined terms and avoid defining things whose everyday meaning is clear – unnecessary defined terms can be confusing for the reader.
- Finally, make sure any definition that you provide is correct and covers everything that you need it to cover – remember, if a term is incorrectly defined, that incorrect definition will be attached to the term throughout the document.

4.3.3 Acronyms

Acronyms are shortened forms of longer words and phrases (for example: WTO is an acronym of World Trade Organisation; EU is an acronym of European Union). Acronyms are similar to defined terms and can help to bring clarity and consistency to your legal writing. They can also help to shorten the length of your sentences and to manage your wordcount.

However, if not used correctly, acronyms can be confusing. As a result, try to stick to acronyms that are widely used and avoid making up too many of your own acronyms.

Example:

- **Helpful use of acronyms:** 'Emily Holloway is a national of the United States (the "US"). While working in the US, she ...' US is a commonly used acronym that the reader is likely to understand.
- **Unhelpful use of acronyms**: 'Emily Holloway is a national of the United States (a "NoUS").' NoUS is not a commonly used acronym and may confuse the reader.

As with defined terms:

- the full meaning of an acronym can be included either within the body of your document or in a separate section or schedule; and
- an acronym can be highlighted in bold or with quotation marks when it appears with its meaning.

Check to ensure if there are any institutional or employer requirements that you should be following.

4.4 Lists

A list will set out a series of connected items that are written consecutively either one after the other or one below the other. In appropriate contexts, lists can be a good way of avoiding a long sentence by splitting up the information into a format that is easy to read and understand.

Example:

Consecutive list: There are three elements to indicate whether a duty of care arises: (1) proximity of the parties; (2) foreseeability of the damage; and (3) an absence of compelling reasons not to find that a duty of care exists.

Listed items below: There are three elements to indicate whether a duty of care arises:
(1) proximity of the parties;
(2) foreseeability of the damage; and
(3) an absence of compelling reasons not to find that a duty of care exists.

A list in your legal writing will not always be appropriate. For example, when you are writing an academic article or an essay for your lecturer you are less likely to use lists, particularly those with bullet points. However, lists can be helpful in other situations where information needs to be displayed in a way that allows it to be identified quickly. Lists are, therefore, useful in more practical documents such as letters of advice and emails.

When items in a list follow one after the other, make sure that you identify each item using a number, letter, bullet point or similar identifying mark. There are two main types of list.

(1) **A list that is a continuous sentence of which the listed items form part:** If a list is part of a continuous sentence you should introduce the list with a colon, put semicolons after each item in the list, start each item in the list with a lower-case letter and only add a full stop at the end of the list. Between the last two items in the list add 'and', 'or', as appropriate.

Example:	Explanation:
There are three elements to indicate whether a duty of care arises:	← Introduce the list with a colon.
(1) proximity of the parties;	← Start each item in the list with a lower-case letter.
(2) foreseeability of the damage; and	← Separate items in the list with semi-colons.
(3) an absence of compelling reasons not to find that a duty of care exists.	← Between the last two items add 'and'/'or'. ← End with a full stop if this is the end of the sentence.

(2) **A list with an introductory statement, but where each item in the list could stand as a separate sentence:** If each item in the list is meant to be read as a complete sentence, start each item with a capital letter and end with a full stop.

Example:	Explanation:
Ms Holloway made the following statements to the police.	← Introductory statement ends in a full stop.
(1) She had received training on how to deal with Caden's haemophilia.	← Each item is a full sentence.
(2) She had not realised the armed men had entered the sports complex.	← Start each item with a capital letter.
(3) She has suffered from depression since the incident.	← End each item with a full stop.

4.5 Quotations

A quotation allows you to repeat the words of another person or entity and to incorporate these into your legal writing. You should always attribute quotations to the original author or speaker. See Chapter 6 for further discussion about plagiarism and the importance of effective citations.

4.5.1 Use of quotations

Including quotations in legal writing can be a helpful way of adding legitimacy to the statements that you are making. Particularly in an academic context, referring to the statements of judges or other legal experts demonstrates to the reader that what you are writing has a basis in scholarship and has not just been made up. Quotations can also be helpful if you want to demonstrate to the reader why a particular statement is incorrect, or if you think an idea or concept was articulated well by someone else.

The extent to which quotations will be relevant in your legal writing will depend on the type of document you are preparing. Quotations are likely to be expected in case notes, essays, academic articles and detailed letters of advice. On the other hand, use of quotations will be less relevant in emails or more practical documents.

4.5.2 Presentation of quotations

How quotations appear in your legal writing will depend on their length.

(1)   **Quotations that are three lines long or less:** Shorter quotations should be incorporated within the body of your text.

If the quotation is incorporated within the middle of a sentence, the first letter of the quotation should be lowercase (add square brackets around the lowercase letter if the original quotation starts with a capital letter). If the quotation is at the beginning of a sentence, the first letter of the quotation should be capitalised (add square brackets around the capital letter if the original quotation starts with a lowercase letter).

Surround these quotations with single (' ') or double (" ") quotation marks. Whichever type of quotation marks you choose, use them consistently throughout the document. If you use single quotation marks, any quotation within a quotation should be surrounded by double quotation marks; if you use double quotation marks, any quotation within a quotation should be surrounded by single quotation marks.

Punctuation should appear outside of the quotation marks, unless that punctuation is itself part of the quotation.[10] The footnote mark should always appear after the closing quotation mark.

> **Example:**
>
> - **Punctuation *outside* quotation marks:** Lord Reid, in *Home Office v Dorset Yacht Co*[11] stated that the chain of causation will be broken unless that act of the third party is something 'very likely to happen'.[12]
>
> - **Quotation within a quotation, punctuation *inside* quotation marks**: In her statement Ms Holloway said, 'I tried to keep calm when the armed man shouted, "I do not want to hurt anyone, but if anyone moves, I will do it". I did not think he would follow through on that threat.'

(2)   **Quotations that are more than three lines long:** Longer quotations should appear as an indented paragraph with an empty line above and below the indented paragraph.

---

[10]   American English adopts a slightly different approach to punctuation in quotations and so commas and full stops go inside the quotation marks in American English, even if they were not part of the original quotation.

[11]   [1970] AC 1004.

[12]   [1970] AC 1004, 1028.

Indented quotations should not be surrounded by quotation marks, although any quotations within the quotation should take single or double quotation marks.

Longer quotations are usually introduced by a colon, but always be mindful of the punctuation that precedes and follows an indented quotation – it must make sense in the context. The footnote mark should always appear after any punctuation at the end of the quotation.

Example:

Nothing more is needed, and nothing less will suffice, as noted by Lord Macmillan:

> The common law has never recognised this subjective standard. If a man's conduct complies with the standard of care of a reasonable person, it does not matter if that falls short of some higher standard of care habitually adopted by himself.[13]

Practical Tip:

Remember, if you change or add anything to a quotation (for example, capitalising the first letter) ensure that you include amendments within square brackets. If you leave one or more words out of a quotation, include ellipses to show that some original text has been removed.

4.5.3 Using quotations effectively in legal writing

(1) **Do not quote material out of context:** Be careful when you are using quoted material that you do not present it out of context. This can occur when the circumstances or material surrounding the quotation are ignored so as to distort the meaning intended by the original author or speaker.

---

[13] *Glasgow Corporation v Muir* [1943] AC 448, 457.

> **Example:**
>
> Ms Holloway once stated, 'I hate children', something that might suggest that she did not care about Caden's safety.
>
> The above use of a quotation would be fine if Emily Holloway made the statement 'I hate children' in the context of looking after children in her care. However, if she was simply reciting the line 'I hate children' for an amateur dramatic version of the movie *Maleficent*, then she clearly did not intend for the statement to have the meaning given to it in the sentence above and to quote it in that way would be to take it out of context.

(2) **Introduce quotations:** It should be clear to the reader how a quotation relates to the document in which it is included. A random quotation in the middle of a document with no explanation as to why it is being used and no words introducing it is unlikely to be very helpful to the reader. Introduce your quotations and blend them into the document – this could be an introduction setting out who you are quoting (for example: 'X noted that, …') or an explanation of what you are quoting (for example: 'In discussing the concept of duty of care towards children, X noted that, …').

(3) **Avoid overuse of quotations:** While quotations can help to support your arguments, you will nevertheless be expected to add some originality to a piece of legal writing. If you write an essay all of which is quotations from other sources, you are unlikely to receive a good grade. You must add something to the discussion, not just quote other people.

The appropriate number of quotations to include in legal writing will always depend on the context and the subject matter about which you are writing. However, strive to only include quotations that add depth to your arguments and elevate your document. Do not include quotations just for the sake of including them.

4.6 Chapter summary

- Good writing should go unnoticed – what you want to avoid is someone noticing poor writing.

- Spend time learning rules of spelling, grammar and punctuation – do not rely on your computer to spot any mistakes.

- Punctuation adds in the pauses, stops, intonation, emphasis and connections that come naturally when sentences are spoken, but which are otherwise absent from written words. Use punctuation to make your legal writing more accessible and engaging.

- Defined terms and acronyms can (if used correctly) help to bring greater consistency to legal writing.

- While lists are not always appropriate in legal writing, they are a simple way to display information.

- The form that quotations take in legal writing will depend on the length of the relevant quotation.

Chapter 5

Legal Writing – Making the Right Impact

Chapter overview:

5.1 Use plain English (and your common sense)
5.2 Appropriate legal writing style
5.3 Impactful sentences and paragraphs
5.4 Presentation and details
5.5 Polishing your legal writing
5.6 Improving your legal writing
5.7 Proofreading checklist
5.8 Chapter summary

5.1 Use plain English (and your common sense)

5.1.1 Plain English

Write using plain language. This does not mean that you should oversimplify your work, or that you should avoid dealing with complex concepts. A document written in plain English must still be correct and it must still include all relevant details. Writing in plain English simply means using language that is straightforward, clear and which can be easily understood by the intended reader. You do not want your reader reaching for a dictionary to try to understand your work – this will frustrate and distract them.

Students (and lawyers) are prone to using elaborate and complicated words and phrases. While this is not wrong, overreliance on convoluted language and old-fashioned turns of phrase can distract the reader, particularly when used incorrectly. This could reduce the readability and impact of your legal writing. Think before you use a complex word – if there is a short, simple word that conveys the same meaning and is appropriate to use in the circumstances, use it.

Example:

Contrast the following two paragraphs, both of which are saying the same thing.

Per the accepted facts, on the day in question, Emily Holloway commenced her journey in the afternoon. The aforementioned Ms Holloway was a passenger in the bus. En route to the sports complex, the aforementioned bus stopped at a supermarket whereupon Ms Holloway exited the vehicle. Whenceforth the other occupants in the bus followed Ms Holloway.	As agreed, on the afternoon of the day in question, Emily Holloway was a passenger in a bus. Before going to the sports complex, the bus stopped at a supermarket. On arrival at the supermarket Ms Holloway and the other occupants of the bus got out.

The advice above does, of course, come with a plea that while you should strive to use plain language, you must also use your common sense while doing so. Use of complex words and phrases is sometimes unavoidable. Different situations will call for a different level of formality, different topics and clients may require the use of particular words and phrases (not all of which would be classified as plain English), different types of written communications will benefit from different levels of complexity. Always think about the intended reader of your writing and be sensitive to his or her expectations.

Practical Tip:

In law, there are certain legal terms that you should not alter into plain English – for example 'duty of care', 'constructive trust' or 'shadow director'. When using such terms in your legal writing, make sure you do so correctly and consistently. You are using these legal terms to convey a specific meaning to the reader.

Set out below is a list of some complex words and phrases commonly used in legal writing, together with simpler equivalents.

Consider before using	Consider using instead
append	attach
aforesaid	above; referred to above
commence	start
foregoing	above; this
for the purpose of	to
hence	therefore
henceforth	going forwards; from now on

Consider before using	Consider using instead
hereafter	after
hereinafter	below
hereinbefore	above
hereto	to this
hereunder	below
in accordance with	under
pertaining to	about
prior to	before
pursuant to	under; because of
subsequent to	after
terminate	end
thereinafter	from then on
thereof	of it
thereto	to it
thereunder	under it
the same	It; *or just identify what it is that you are referring to*
whereupon	after which

Practical Tip:

Read what you have written out loud. Writing that uses plain language should be clear and easy to read. If you find yourself stumbling over a word or sentence, consider whether it could be simplified without changing its meaning.

5.1.2 Latin words and phrases

Latin words and phrases, such as *res ipsa loquitur*, *actus reus*, *mutatis mutandis* and *pari passu*, are used frequently in court documents and legal contracts. In such circumstances these words and phrases are used because they have specific legal meanings that do not neatly translate into English or because their usage is part of market practice in specific contexts. Some styles of footnoting in academic writing also use Latin words as directions, such as *supra, infra, et al*. If these circumstances are relevant to your piece of legal writing, you should generally follow the established practice. Latin words and phrases are typically italicised, but this will again depend on the house style that you are following.[1]

---

[1] Some house styles only require italicisation of less commonly used Latin words or phrases.

Outside of the above circumstances, avoid using Latin words and phrases. Using Latin in your legal writing can be difficult to get right, may confuse the reader and could result in you making grammatical errors. Set out below is a list of commonly used Latin words and phrases and the plain English alternatives that you might want to consider using.

Consider before using	Consider using instead
ab initio	from the start
ad infinitum	forever
bona fide	in good faith
de facto	in reality
de jure	by law; rightfully
inter alia	among other things; including
per	in accordance with; by
per annum	a year
per se	by itself
prima facie	on its face

5.1.3   Industry jargon

Industry jargon is specialised words or expressions that are used and understood by a particular profession or group of people (for example, 'due diligence',[2] 'hard copy',[3] 'tick and tie'[4]). Industry jargon can have a place in legal writing but be careful when using it. You should be confident that your intended reader is likely to understand it. If you use industry jargon in a context where the reader does not understand it, this could lead to confusion and misunderstanding – something that must be avoided in legal writing. In practice, careful use of industry jargon is likely to be most relevant once you enter a professional environment and become more specialised in your field.

When appropriate, use industry jargon sparingly and sensibly. If you are in any doubt about the use of a piece of industry jargon, consider excluding it or providing an explanation of it the first time you use it.

---

[2]   In a commercial law context this refers to research conducted ahead of entering into an agreement or transaction.

[3]   Used in the legal and business professions to refer to the physical copy of a document rather than the electronic version.

[4]   Used in the legal and auditing professions to refer to the process by which auditors confirm that figures in a document are based on, or taken from, a company's financial statements or internal financial records.

5.2 Appropriate legal writing style

5.2.1 Consider the purpose and intended reader of your writing

All good legal writing requires some level of planning. Even a short email will benefit from you taking a moment to consider why you are sending it and how best to convey your message to the intended recipient. Planning will also help you to take the research that you have conducted and present it in a clear and logical way.

How you plan and structure your legal writing will be influenced by the purpose and the intended reader of that writing. A client who wants a quick answer on the current status of a negotiation does not want (nor have time to read) an in-depth discussion of the relevant legal principles. On the other hand, your lecturer who has assigned you an essay question dealing with a complex legal issue does not want a brief high-level overview. He or she wants you to analyse the law, to discuss the legal authorities and to reflect on the implications of the law.

Before you start writing, therefore, you must clearly identify the purpose and intended reader of your writing. In doing so, consider the following.

- Why are you undertaking this piece of legal writing and are you using the most appropriate format?
- What information does the reader want from you – what does he or she want to know?
- What information does the reader already know and what expertise does he or she have? This will impact on the extent to which the reader will understand specialist terms and concepts – avoid assuming too much knowledge.
- How quickly does the reader want the information? This will determine how you present your legal writing. For example, someone who wants an answer quickly might benefit from a clear summary at the top of a document that provides the answer, rather than being forced to search for the answer in pages of text.
- What does the reader want to do with the information? A lecturer will be reading your essay with the intention of determining the most appropriate grade. A client or supervisor at work might want the information to prepare a presentation or to use as speaking notes for a call.

Only once you have identified your reader and reflected on their expectations will you be able to decide how formal your legal writing should be, how much information to provide and how best to present that information.

5.2.2 Keep your tone professional

While you should aim to write in plain English, avoid adopting a tone in your legal writing that is too informal or overly familiar. Whether you are writing an essay for your lecturer, an internal memo for your supervisor or an advice email for a client, treat what you are doing as a piece of professional writing. Remember, this is a piece of writing on which you are being evaluated. The tone that you adopt in legal writing should not, therefore, be the same as the one that you would use when chatting with your friends. As a result, avoid using clichés, slang, emotional language, hyperbole or lazy adjectives.

- **Clichés:** Clichés are expressions that are so overused that they lose their meaning and using them could make your legal writing appear lacking in original thought. This does not, of course, mean that clichés are not used widely in legal writing today. There is a range of commonly used clichés that you may come across, such 'bitter irony', 'cards on the table', 'in the weeds', 'in the pipeline'. Use of these expressions is a practice that is best avoided. In most cases, using clichés adds little to your legal writing.
- **Slang:** Including slang or very informal words and expressions is unprofessional and should always be avoided in legal writing (unless you are including a direct quotation in which it is used). Slang is often generational and while you may understand what a particular word means, your lecturer, supervisor or client may not. This type of casual language detracts from the strength of your legal writing.
- **Inappropriately emotional language:** Students sometimes use emotional or inflammatory language in their legal writing – for example: 'Ms Holloway's *appalling* disregard for Caden's medical condition', or 'the judge's decision was *utterly outrageous*'. Emotional language can be helpful when trying to build a personal connection with the reader. However, in legal writing such language risks coming across as unprofessional and lacking in poise and control. Keep the tone of your

writing calm and neutral, and avoid subjective outbursts of emotion.

- **Hyperbole and lazy adjectives:** Finally, you should generally avoid using hyperbole, overstatements or lazy adjectives in your legal writing – for example, 'the best', 'unrivalled', 'world-leading'.[5]

Adopting a professional tone in legal writing is particularly easy to forget in email correspondence. See Chapter 7 for guidance on how to prepare emails.

> **Practical Tip:**
>
> Be sensible when it comes to the correct tone for your legal writing. Legal writing will always be formal and professional, but you will need to judge for yourself what level of formality is required in a particular situation. A submission to court will likely be more formal than an email to a client with whom you have a good working relationship.

5.2.3 Refer to judges correctly

In Ireland and in England and Wales, how you refer to judges in writing is different from how you refer to them orally.

Ireland

In Ireland, judges are usually referred to in writing by their surname followed by 'J', 'CJ' or 'P', as appropriate (depending on their role).

> **Example:**
>
> Mr Justice Frank Clarke, Chief Justice, is written as Clark CJ
> Ms Justice Mary Irvine, President of the High Court, is written as Irvine P
> Ms Justice Úna Ní Raifeartaigh is written as Ní Raifeartaigh J
> Ms Justice Elizabeth Dunne and Mr Justice John MacMenamin (together) are written as Dunne and MacMenamin JJ

---

[5] In *Maire Sheehy v Board of Management of Killaloe Convent Primary School* [2019] IEHC 456 [96], Ní Raifeartaigh J commented on the use of exaggeration by a barrister in the case, noting that '[t]he subsequent reactions of Ms. Varley and Ms. Needham as set out in the correspondence described appears to me to be rather excessive, but so too was the position of the applicant, whose counsel before me engaged in considerable hyperbole concerning the matter.'

England and Wales

In England and Wales, the way judges are referred to in writing will depend on a number of factors, including the court in which they sit.

Supreme Court	The written format of Supreme Court judges' titles will typically take the following form: 'Lord/Lady [*surname*] JSC'.
	'JSC' will become 'PSC' for the President of the Supreme Court and 'DPSC' for the Deputy President of the Supreme Court
	Example:
	The Right Hon Lady Arden of Heswall DBE is written as Lady Arden JSC
	The Right Hon Lord Reed of Allermuir, President of the Supreme Court, is written as Lord Reed PSC
	The Right Hon Lord Hodge, Deputy President of the Supreme Court, is written as Lord Hodge DPSC
Court of Appeal	The written format of Court of Appeal judges' titles will typically take the following form: '[*surname*] LJ'
	Example:
	Lady Justice Nicola Davies is written as Davies LJ
	Lord Justice Rabinder Singh is written as Singh LJ
Queen's Bench Division	The written format of Queen's Bench Division judges' titles will typically take the following form: '[*surname*] J'
	Example:
	Ms Justice Elisabeth Laing is written as Laing J
	Mr Justice Edward Pepperall is written as Pepperall J

5.3 Impactful sentences and paragraphs

5.3.1 Keep sentences short and clear

Good legal writing is precise, clear and unambiguous. Keeping your sentences short and your language appropriately simple should make your legal writing easier to read.[6] This is because there is only so much information that a reader can process in one go. When sentences are long and complicated there is a risk that the reader could miss a key point or must read the sentence multiple times in order to understand it.

While this does not mean that you should cut all your sentences down so that they are basic and abrupt, you should strive to make

---

6 Iain Morley, *The Devil's Advocate* (3rd edn, Sweet & Maxwell 2015) 101.

your sentences as clear as possible. This can be achieved in several ways.

- Include **one main idea or concept in each sentence**, rather than dealing with multiple points at the same time.

Example:	
Contrast the following two paragraphs, both of which are saying the same thing.	
Ms Holloway, who is a 25 year-old basketball coach, was in a bus on the way home, although her mother had offered to give her a lift that day, since she had a new car, but Ms Holloway declined and instead took the team bus.	Ms Holloway is a 25 year-old basketball coach. One Saturday in September she was on a bus on the way home. Her mother had offered to drive Ms Holloway in her new car, but Ms Holloway had declined the offer and instead took the team bus.

- Consider how **punctuation can be used to break down long sentences** into ones that are more accessible to the reader. A long sentence could, for example, be broken down into two shorter sentences, or a subsidiary point could be included within parentheses to bring the main idea to the reader's attention. Read the sentence out loud – this could help you to identify where it could naturally be broken into two or more sentences.
- **Omit unnecessary or redundant words**. A sentence should include no unnecessary words. When you are editing a sentence, consider whether every word used contributes to the overall meaning of that sentence. You may be surprised how often you use words or phrases that can simply be deleted without changing the meaning of the sentence. When editing for unnecessary words consider the following.
    - (a) **Tautology:** Tautology is saying the same thing twice using different words. You can generally delete one of the words without altering the meaning of the sentence.

> **Example:**
>
> - 'True facts'. Facts are, by their nature, true. You can delete reference to 'true' without changing the meaning of the sentence.
> - 'In my opinion, I think the judge was wrong'. By referring to your opinion, you are indicating that this is what you think. You do not also need to say 'I think'.
> - 'Combine together'. Combining something brings it together. You can simply delete 'together' here.

(b) **Unnecessary overemphasis:** Overemphasising things by using qualifying words (for example: 'very', 'rather', 'totally', 'completely') is usually unnecessary in legal writing.[7] A qualifying word modifies the impact of the word that follows it. Qualifying words should not be used to modify absolute adjectives and they should be used sparingly when modifying other types of words.

> **Example:**
>
> - 'Ms Holloway is *utterly* confused by what happened to Mr Goldsmith.' 'Utterly' can be removed.
> - 'Mr Goldsmith is *very* determined to recover.' 'Very' can be removed.
> - 'The decision of the court was *completely* unanimous.' Unanimous is an absolute adjective and cannot be modified (that is, there are not grades of unanimity, something is unanimous, or it is not).

(c) **Redundant words and phrases:** Certain words and phrases are used frequently in writing but ultimately add little to the meaning of the sentence. These include 'the fact that/is', 'clearly', 'of course', 'it is important to add'. Try to edit these out of your legal writing.

5.3.2 Vary sentence length

While short sentences will help with the readability of your legal writing, repeatedly using short, punchy sentences can sound aggressive, monotonous and boring. You should, therefore, aim for

---

[7] Strunk and White went so far as to describe qualifiers as 'leeches that infest the pond of prose, sucking the blood of words', William Strunk and EB White, *The Elements of Style* (4th edn, Longman 2000) 73.

an average sentence length of about 15–20 words, but be prepared to vary the length between sentences. A longer sentence that is clear and unambiguous can be balanced out with a shorter following sentence. Varying sentence length will help your legal writing to be more engaging.

5.3.3 Avoid long, complicated paragraphs

Like sentences, your paragraphs should be clear and coherent. Paragraphs provide the reader with a natural break between concepts and give that reader a chance to take in what has just been discussed. A piece of legal writing that is a single uninterrupted paragraph might not only be daunting for the reader, but could be difficult to follow.

Paragraph lengths will vary. In order to keep paragraph length manageable, avoid writing in paragraphs that cover multiple subjects, themes or ideas. As is the case with sentences, try to stick to one main concept in each paragraph.

5.3.4 Be aware of narrative perspective

As you prepare for a piece of legal writing, you will need to consider what the intended reader wants from the piece. Do they want your opinion? Do they want you to provide a neutral analysis of the law? Do they want you to write a letter on their behalf? This will determine from whose narrative perspective you should be writing.

The first-person narrative uses the word 'I' and expresses the author's opinion. There are some situations where this first-person narrative is appropriate in legal writing. For example, if your lecturer has asked for your opinion on a judge's reasoning in a case.

More frequently, however, use of the first-person narrative is not appropriate and can appear too casual. Unless you are asked to express your opinion in a piece of legal writing, you should generally avoid doing so. In a moot, for example, you are advancing arguments on behalf of your client, not in your personal capacity. When providing legal advice to a client of the law firm where you work, you are representing the firm, not presenting yourself as a legal authority. In each of these situations, you should not express personal opinions and should avoid using first-person subjective phrases such as 'I think …', 'I believe …' or 'I want …'. Instead, consider using more neutral and objective language.

First-person phrases	Consider using instead
I am sure this piece of legislation is not applicable.	This piece of legislation is not applicable
In this note, *I will analyse* the relevance of *novus actus interveniens* in contemporary Irish law.	This note will analyse the relevance of *novus actus interveniens* in contemporary Irish law.
I believe that my client was correct.	It is submitted that Ms Holloway is correct (or simply) Ms Holloway is correct.
In conclusion, *I would argue* that the case has now been overruled.	In conclusion, it is arguable that the case has now been overruled.

5.3.5 Prefer the active voice (but do not ignore the passive voice)

Using the active voice in your legal writing is more concise and can sound more assured and persuasive than the passive voice. Readers understand sentences in the active voice more quickly and easily. This is because the active voice follows how we think and process information.

In a sentence where the verb is in the active voice, the subject of the sentence *acts upon* the object. When a verb is in the passive voice, the object becomes the subject of the sentence and that subject *is acted upon*.

> **Example:**
>
> **Active voice:** The armed man [*subject*] threw [*verb*] the grenade [*object*].
>
> **Passive voice:** The grenade [*subject*] was thrown [*verb*] by the armed man [*preposition phrase*].

There are a number of issues with using the passive voice.

- **It can be confusing and vague:** In a sentence that uses the passive voice, the actor can be removed from the sentence and the sentence will still make sense. For example: 'Emily was narrowly missed' – here 'by the grenade' has been removed. This cannot be done when using the active voice. For example: 'Narrowly misses Emily' is not a complete sentence. By allowing the writer to remove the actor of a sentence, the passive voice could lead to confusion and may not provide the reader with all of the necessary details.

- **It can make sentences longer as you need to use more words:** When using the passive voice, you may have to add additional words in order to construct a sentence. In the example above, the sentence in the passive voice needs the addition of 'was' and 'by'.

While you should generally write in the active voice, there are occasions when the passive voice is appropriate.

- **When the subject of the sentence is unknown:** If you do not have all of the facts and so you do not know who or what acted on the subject of the sentence, you may need to use the passive voice. For example: 'Caden was hit on the arm' (if you do not know who or what hit him).
- **When the action in the sentence is more important than the actor:** If the reader is not interested in the actor of the sentence and is, rather, concerned with action, the passive voice may be useful in focusing the reader's attention. For example: 'No evidence was found'. Here, what is important to the reader is that no evidence was found, not that you were the one who carried out this check.
- **When you want to sound more objective, or you do not want to refer to the actor:** The passive voice has a more detached, objective quality to it. This can be useful if you want to avoid being seen to ascribe blame for the action, or if you deliberately want to avoid identifying the actor. For example: 'The allegation is denied', rather than 'The allegation is denied by Ms Holloway'. Here, you are removing Ms Holloway from the sentence and diverting attention away from her as the actor.

5.3.6 Write in the positive, rather than the negative

Try to write your sentences using positive language, rather than negative language. Positive sentences are more direct and may be shorter than negative sentences. They can project greater confidence and conviction in what is being said. Using positive language also makes legal writing easier to read as the reader will often convert a negative sentence into a positive one in order to understand it – by writing in the positive, you avoid this extra step.

The keyword to look out for when trying to avoid using negative language is 'not'. When you find yourself using 'not' in a sentence, consider whether the sentence can be rephrased to recast it as a positive.

> **Example:**
>
> - Contrast 'persons other than Ms Holloway may *not* address the court at this time' with 'only Ms Holloway may address the court at this time'.
> - Contrast 'she was *not* usually on time to training' with 'she was usually late to training'.
> - Contrast 'the court did *not* accept the barrister's submissions because she had *not* submitted the evidence on time' with 'the court rejected the barrister's statements because she had submitted them too late'.

5.3.7 Use gender-neutral language (if appropriate)

When you make a statement in legal writing that does not relate to a specific person or to a group of people, keep the language gender-neutral. This means that you should try to avoid gender-specific references, such as his, her, he, she.

Referring to people generally will usually require some gender-specific references. How you do this is a matter of personal (or institutional/employer) style. Section 18(b) Interpretation Act 2005 provides that use of the masculine form of a word should be read as including the feminine and vice versa.[8] However, you may prefer to use more gender-balanced references, such as:

- using plurals (for example: 'They are expected to act reasonably');
- repeating nouns so that you do not need to refer to a gender (for example: 'If a coach does not act reasonably, that coach will be held liable…'); or
- using he/she or s/he (for example: 'He/she will be found to have been negligent').

Once you enter the professional world, it is a good idea to check which approach your employer prefers and adapt your legal writing accordingly.

If you are talking about a person and you know that person is male or female, then you should use gender-specific wording.

5.3.8 Be consistent

Consistency in language is key in legal writing. Consistency helps with clarity and avoids confusion. As a result, the general approach in legal writing should be that you should use words

---

[8] Section 18(b)(i) and (ii) Interpretation Act 2005.

and expressions consistently throughout a document. Do not be afraid of repetition. If you are inconsistent in how you describe something, this can leave the reader wondering whether you are talking about distinct things. This is not something the reader should have to work out.

> **Example:**
>
> If you referred to your client as 'Ms Holloway' for the first five pages of your document, then to suddenly start referring to her as 'the coach' on page six could be confusing to the reader and may cause him or her to wonder whether this is a different person.

The need for precision and consistency will become even more important if you enter the legal profession where vagueness and uncertainty in language could have significant implications for your client.

> **Practical Tip:**
>
> A useful way of maintaining consistency throughout a piece of legal writing is to use defined terms. By using defined terms, you can define concepts, parties or things that you will be referring to repeatedly in your document. Every subsequent reference to that concept, party or thing will simply be a reference to the defined term. This will reduce the risk of inconsistent language. See Section 4.3.2 above for more discussion of defined terms.

Consistency of tense is also important in legal writing. Take a moment to consider what tense you should be writing in. This will depend on the purpose of your legal writing. For example, are you writing a case note about a judgment that has already been issued, are you providing advice on a potential future change in legislation, or are you commenting on the current legal position? Once you have confirmed the correct tense, avoid switching between tenses within a document without good reason.

5.4 Presentation and details

5.4.1 Word counts

Particularly in an academic context, you may have been set a maximum (and perhaps a minimum) word count for a piece of legal writing. Outside of academia, prescriptive word counts are less common (but not unheard of). Even if no maximum word count has been set, you should still aim to write as clearly and concisely as you can.

When you have been set a maximum word count, you should adhere to this word count. A failure to do so could result in you being penalised either through marks being deducted based on the number of excess words or because the lecturer simply stops reading after the maximum word count has been reached. Because of this, you should be vigilant when it comes to word count. Always make sure that you confirm the following.

- **What is included in the word count.** You should confirm whether footnotes, bibliography, title page, list of abbreviations, list of definitions, tables, and lists of statutes and case law are included or excluded from the word count. If it is not obvious from the instructions provided, check.
- **Whether the maximum word count is strict.** Some third-level institutions allow an amount of flexibility in the set word count, for example, the instructions may confirm that there will be no penalty if the final word count of an essay is 10 percent over or 10 percent under the set word count. Do not assume this flexibility will always apply and check before implementing it in your legal writing.

Write with the maximum word count in mind. While you can always cut down what you have written in the editing process, you must be realistic as you write – if you have been asked to write a 5,000-word case note, there is no point in your first draft being 25,000 words – this is just a waste of your time since most of what you have written will need to be removed. With that said, however, your first draft is likely to be somewhat over the maximum word count. This is not a bad thing, you will find that the editing process of reducing your word count will make your writing more engaging, concise and focused. To help bring your word count down:

- **use the tools discussed in this book** – make careful use of abbreviations, defined terms, writing in the active voice, short sentences and impactful paragraphs;
- **remove unnecessary information** – make sure that everything included in your legal writing is contributing to the overall text. For example, do you need to give so much detail about the background of a marginal case?; and
- **remove repetition** – if you have said something once in a document, you probably do not need to say it again. If you do, you can cross-refer back to the earlier discussion.

While concise writing is important, you should also try to avoid coming in well below the maximum word count (and you may be penalised for doing so). The maximum word count has been set because that is what the person who set it thinks is needed to deal with the subject of the legal writing. If you find that you are significantly short of the maximum word count check to make sure that you have provided enough detail, that you have dealt with all of the relevant material and that you have answered all questions asked.

> **Practical Tip:**
>
> Your assignments have word limits for a reason – they tell you the amount of work the lecturer thinks you need to do to demonstrate that you have understood the issues at stake. If the maximum word count is small, this indicates that you do not need to include huge amounts of information in the essay. Therefore, you can plan to focus on only the most relevant sources and points of analysis.

5.4.2 Formatting and layout

Document formatting refers to how the document looks on the page. Your legal writing should look like a piece of professional work that you are proud of. Avoid your excellent legal research and planning being let down by confusing or inappropriate written presentation.

The required formatting for a piece of legal writing will often be dictated either by the person who assigns you the work (for example, your lecturer) or by the house style of your employer or the publisher for whom you are writing. An organisation's house style is that organisation's preferred manner of written presentation and layout of written material. By way of example, law firms will often have very prescriptive requirements as to how documents are formatted, including font size and style, heading style and line spacing. If there is a house style in place or you have been asked to follow a formatting style, you must familiarise yourself with it and follow it. Do not just pick and choose elements that you like.

If you have not been given formatting specifications to follow, you will have a little more control over the presentation of your legal writing. Nevertheless, you should still follow a formatting style that is professional – this is not an opportunity for you to display your creative flair. Use your chosen style consistently throughout your piece of work.

Set out below are some standard formatting specifications.

	Formatting	Discussion
1.	Font style	Use a font that is easy to read. Times New Roman or Arial are commonly used fonts.
2.	Font size	Text: Make sure the text is easy to read. 11-point or 12-point font size is usually appropriate. Footnote or endnotes: These will usually be one or two font sizes smaller than the text of the main body. This is usually 10-point font size.
3.	Page numbering	Pages should generally be numbered, with page numbers centred in the footer of each page.
4.	Line spacing	Double (2.0) and one-and-a-half line spacing (1.5) will make your written work easier to read.
5.	Text alignment	Text whose alignment is justified (where the text spacing is adjusted so that text touches both the left and right margins) can make writing look more polished.
6.	Margins	Use standard margins (2.54 cm on each margin).
7.	Emphasis	If you want to emphasise a word, do so in italics or bold.
8.	Use of colour	Text should generally be black and printed on white paper. Colour may be used for images, graphs, charts and diagrams.
9.	Paragraphs	Separate paragraphs, either by including an empty line between paragraphs or by indenting the first line of each new paragraph.

5.4.3 Headings and signposting

Headings and sub-headings should reflect the content of the paragraphs that follow and should be used to inform readers as to what is to come and to encourage them to keep reading.

Headings and sub-headings act as signposts to help guide the reader along the path that you are laying for him or her. By including clear and relevant headings and sub-headings, you will make it easier for the reader to navigate your written work and to understand why you have reached your conclusion. It also allows the reader to move more easily between sections of your writing and to understand how each section ties into the wider purpose of your written work.

Neutral headings and sub-headings are appropriate in legal

writing where you are presenting the legal position or providing client advice. However, in legal writing in which you propose various arguments (such as an academic article or an essay set by your lecturer), you may use headings and sub-headings as an opportunity to emphasise the point or argument that you are making. Rather than simply including neutral headings and sub-headings, therefore, consider using argumentative headings and sub-headings in legal writing in which arguments are being made. These will clearly and immediately tell the reader what argument is being dealt with in the subsequent paragraphs.[9] In this way, you are using your headings and sub-headings to reinforce the persuasiveness of your legal writing.

> **Example:**
>
> Rather than the heading being neutral, such as '**Causation**', clearly state the argument that is being made, such as '**The Chain of Causation was not broken**'.

The formatting of headings and sub-headings should be consistent throughout your piece of legal writing. All of your main headings should, therefore, follow the same style (for example, bold and numbered using 1, 2, 3 etc) and each level of sub-heading should similarly follow a consistent style (for example, italicised and numbered using 1.1, 1.2, 2.1, 2.2 etc).

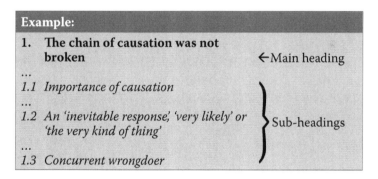

> **Example:**
>
> 1. **The chain of causation was not broken** ← Main heading
> ...
> *1.1 Importance of causation*
> ...
> *1.2 An 'inevitable response', 'very likely' or 'the very kind of thing'* } Sub-headings
> ...
> *1.3 Concurrent wrongdoer*

Inconsistent formatting of headings and sub-headings can lead to reader confusion as it may not be clear how various sections of your writing relate to each other.

5.4.4 Cases

Case names should be italicised in the main body of your text and

---

[9] Andrew Goodman, *Effective Written Advocacy* (2nd edn, Wildy, Simmonds & Hill Publishing 2012), 60.

in footnotes or endnotes. Make sure that you *do not* also italicise the citation for a case, the footnote mark or any following punctuation – these should all be unitalicised.

The 'v' between the parties should always be lowercase. Whether the 'v' is followed by a full stop is a matter of personal preference or may be covered by the house style you are required to follow. Whatever approach you choose, make sure you do so consistently throughout your piece of legal writing. For more information on referencing cases, see Section 6.3.1 below.

5.4.5 Page numbers

Including page numbers in your documents helps the reader to navigate the document. It also ensures that your document can easily be pieced back together in the right order should the pages get mixed up.

For documents that have more than one page, therefore, make sure that you include page numbers. Follow any formatting specifications that you are given and check any house style available when you are formatting page numbers in your documents. In the absence of such details, include page numbers in the centre footer of your document and ensure that they are the same font as the body of your document.

5.4.6 Numbers, times and dates

(1) **Numbers:** Consult any relevant house style for information on how to present numbers. In the absence of such guidance, consider writing numbers above 10 in figures (for example, 1,604, 2,056…) and numbers 10 and below in letters (for example, one, two, three…).

The exceptions to the approach of writing numbers above 10 in figures are when:
- the number starts a sentence (for example, 'The chain of causation was not broken. Eleven things must be considered…');
- using numbers for page references, section references and paragraph numbers;
- you are setting out a list of numbers where some are lower and higher than 10 (for example, 'In the last four years, there were 2, 99, 45 and 3 cases, respectively');
- using numbers for a sum of money (for example, €3); and

- using numbers for percentages (for example, 2% or 2 per cent).

(2) **Times:** Write times consistently – if you use the 24-hour clock for one reference to time, make sure all times that you refer to are expressed in this format (for example, 17:00, 19:30). If you are writing an email to a client, or are setting up a meeting, consider whether it would be helpful to include the time zone (for example, 'the meeting is scheduled for 15:30 (Dublin time)').

(3) **Dates:** Write dates consistently. Consult any relevant house style for information on how to present dates. In the absence of such guidance, consider writing the day in figures, the month in letters and the year in figures (for example, 5 December 2020).

5.5 Polishing your legal writing

5.5.1 Optics and attention to detail

Do not underestimate how important optics are when it comes to your legal writing. How your piece of written work *looks* is an important part of the impact it has on the reader. This is the first impression that piece of work will have on the reader – a sloppy, poorly laid out document risks creating a bad impression. In contrast, a piece of work that is well laid out, properly formatted and easy to navigate will start you off on the right foot with the reader. Take, for example, the following two examples. They both say the same thing, but one is well presented, while the other one is poorly presented and full of typos – think about the impression each leaves with the reader.

Example:

Good presentation
Ryan J was mistaken in holding that Ms Holloway was not responsible for the acts of the armed man, because:

a) authorities, both from this jurisdiction, and from England, state that a defendant will be liable for the act or omission of a third party where that act or omission was an inevitable response, very likely or the very thing against which the defendant ought, reasonably, to have guarded; and

b) even if Ms Holloway cannot be held solely liable for the relevant injuries, she is, in the alternative, a concurrent wrongdoer under the terms of s 11(1) of the Civil Liability Act 1961.

Poor presentation
Ryan Judge was mistaken in holding that Ms Holooway was not responsible for the act's of armed man, because authorities, both from this jurisdiction, and from England, state That an accused will be liable for the act or omission third party where that act or Omission was an inevitable response, Very likely or the very thing against which the defendent ought, reasonably, to have guarded; and even if Ms Honolulu cannot be held solely liable for the relevant injuries she is in the alternative a concurrent wrongdoer under the terms of sll(l) of the
civil liability ACT 1961.

Attention to detail is an important feature of well-presented work. Having good attention to detail will help you to thoroughly review and proofread your work, picking out even the smallest inaccuracies, mistakes and inconsistencies. Your attention to detail is something that you can improve, but you must work at it. Make sure that you spend time checking and correcting your work. Focus on reading each sentence carefully. Then take a step back and consider your work as a single piece of writing – make sure it is internally consistent in terms of substance, structure and appearance.

Practical Tip:

While attention to detail and the proper presentation of your written work are certainly important at third level, they will be even more important once you enter a professional environment. Accuracy and avoiding errors are essential skills for lawyers and non-lawyers. Your supervisor and clients do not want to be presented with a piece of written work that is hard to read, full of errors or poorly laid out – it is *your* role to address these points before submitting your work.

5.5.2 Refining your legal writing

The first draft of a piece of legal writing should never be the final version that you submit. Once you have finished the first draft, you then need to refine and polish your document. This involves editing and proofreading your work. Make sure that you give yourself enough time to do both – the refining process should not be left until the last minute as this will result in it being rushed.

(1) **Editing and revising your work:** When you edit your legal writing, you re-read your work with the aim of improving its content, clarity and structure.

With any maximum word count in mind, read your piece of legal writing carefully. Consider whether it serves its purpose and whether it does so clearly and succinctly. As part of the editing process, you will need to check the following.

- **Purpose:** Consider whether the document does what it was supposed to do. Does it answer the question(s) asked? Does it deliver the information needed? Does it provide the reader with the explanations sought? It can be easy to focus on individual sentences and paragraphs in a piece of legal writing and in doing so to lose sight of what that writing is intended to do.
- **Clarity to the reader:** Not only should a piece of legal writing fulfil its intended purpose, but it should do so in a way that will be understood by its intended reader. Consider your reader and his or her expectations.
- **Content:** Make sure that the information included is correct – double check points that you are unsure about.
- **Structure:** Ensure that your legal writing follows a logical structure that will make sense to the reader. Consider the length of your sentences – avoid overly long sentences. Confirm that each paragraph contains one main idea. Use headings and sub-headings to help define a document's structure and aid reader comprehension.
- **Flow throughout the document:** There should be a logical flow between concepts and paragraphs in your legal writing. Do not jump between concepts or include paragraphs that are unconnected to those around them. This will confuse the reader. If necessary, guide the reader from one paragraph or concept to the next using signposting and headings.
- **Unnecessary words/phrases:** Remember to use plain English – rework complicated sentences or paragraphs to improve readability and omit unnecessary words.

(2) Proofreading: When you proofread your legal writing, you read the near final version of a document to check for errors.

Although proofreading your work will be one of the last things that you do before submitting or sending your work, it is a vital stage in effective and impactful legal writing. It is also a stage that is so often rushed or missed completely. Proofreading helps you to produce a polished and accurate piece of work. As such, it is a way of preventing your hard work from being overshadowed by careless mistakes.

When you proofread a piece of legal writing, read the document slowly. Look carefully for spelling or grammatical mistakes, inconsistent references to people, courts, places or concepts, incorrect use of capitalisation, and formatting errors. You should also check your footnotes (or endnotes) to ensure these are correct, consistently presented and (in the case of footnotes) on the correct page.

> **Practical Tip:**
>
> For longer pieces of legal writing, **print out a copy of the document**. Proofreading on a computer screen can be difficult and you are more likely to miss errors than if you proofread the document in hard copy.
>
> It is also a good idea to ask someone else to proofread your work as he or she may pick up on errors that you have missed. This is particularly relevant for important pieces of legal writing, such as an essay or a letter of advice (subject to client confidentiality restrictions).

Set out below is a list of steps to work through when proofreading your work. Section 5.8 below sets these out as a checklist that you can use for your own legal writing. You may want to add to this checklist where you are aware of some aspect of your writing style that needs particular attention (for example, perhaps you frequently write dates inconsistently or you mix up the words 'judgment' and 'judgement').

Remember to check	Discussion
Use of **proper nouns**, in particular the names of people, places, cases and courts	This is information that you should double, if not triple, check as part of your proofreading. It looks extremely sloppy if you spell a judge's or your client's name incorrectly. Make a specific effort to check these as it can be very easy to skip over this information as part of your proofread.

Remember to check	Discussion
Citations and other **references**	Make sure that you have cited any cases fully and correctly – double check the citation.
	Have you provided a full and correct reference for anything that you are quoting or paraphrasing?
	Are footnotes on the correct page?
Consistent use of **defined terms**	Check to make sure that you have provided an explanation of each defined term, that you have capitalised the first letter of each defined term and that you have used defined terms consistently – check to make sure that you have not referred to something that you have defined using different terminology.
Use of **complete sentences**	Have you inadvertently missed out words in your sentences? If you do not pay close attention in your proofreading, you may not notice the omission of words (particularly small supporting words like 'and' or 'the'). Reading sentences out loud can help you to catch incomplete sentences.
Correct use of **punctuation**	Check use of apostrophes, commas, full stops, colons, semi-colons and other punctuation.
	Ctrl-F (Command-F for Mac users) '(' and ')' to make sure there is an even number of parentheses (an uneven number means you have missed out a parenthesis somewhere in your document).
Spelling	Watch out not only for words that are clearly misspelled, but also check for words that your computer's spell-check may have missed – refer to the table of such words in Section 4.1.2 above.
Consistent presentation of **headings, numbered items, lists, bullet points**.	Read each heading in your piece of legal writing (it can be easy to skim over these). Is each the correct heading for the section of writing that follows?
	Look at how you have presented headings, lists and other numbered or bullet-pointed information. Is this all consistent (e.g. if you start your first heading with (A) in bold italics, do all subsequent headings of the same level follow this format?).

Remember to check	Discussion
Check the **formatting**	Are there any specific instructions that you have been given in terms of how your legal writing should be formatted (e.g. what font, font size, line spacing are you expected to use)? If so, check to make sure these instructions have been followed consistently throughout your work. If you have not been given specific formatting instructions, you should still consider the formatting of your work – how does it look optically? Is the font style and size consistent? Are paragraphs evenly spaced? This may not seem important, but a properly formatted piece of legal writing helps to create the right impression with the reader.

5.6 Improving your legal writing

5.6.1 Feedback

Seek out feedback on your legal writing, where appropriate. Read any comments that are given to you by the person reading your work. Reflect on these comments and consider what errors the reader has picked up on.

Where you have submitted to a lecturer or your supervisor at work and you are unsure about the comments that have been made, ask if you can schedule a meeting to run through these comments and to discuss how you can improve your legal writing skills. You may also find other helpful resources at third level or in your workplace, such as writing centres or courses on legal writing.

5.6.2 The importance of practising and reading examples

Do remember that you cannot expect the reader to highlight every error that you make in a document. Nor will some readers provide you with any feedback since it is not their job to comment on the strength of your writing. It is, ultimately, your responsibility to improve your legal writing.

The best way to improve your legal writing is to consciously and deliberately practise these skills – think about the words that you are using, your sentence and paragraph structures, the optics of your writing. The more you do this, the more natural the implementation of these skills will be.

In addition to practising your own legal writing, you should also try to read examples of good (and poor) legal writing. This will give you examples to draw on, examples of what to avoid, and techniques that you can try out in your own legal writing. Objectively reading examples of other people's legal writing can be one of the most useful ways of appreciating what works and what does not work in a piece of legal writing.

5.7 Chapter summary

- Avoid using complicated or archaic words and phrases. Writing is only effective if it can be understood.

- Try to assume the right tone for your legal writing – remember, legal writing should be professional.

- Effective legal writing is about more than what you write, it is also about how you write – keep your sentences short, vary sentence length, avoid long, complicated paragraphs, be aware of narrative perspective, use the active voice, write in the positive, use gender-neutral language and be consistent.

- Consider the presentation of your written work – formatting that is clear and easy to read, a logical layout, headings and signposts, and page numbers make it easier for the reader to follow what you have written.

- Proofread your work – your legal writing should never be completed before you have proofread it at least once.

5.8 Proofreading checklist

Photocopy this page and use it when proofreading your work – tick off each point as you check it. While not every point will be relevant to each piece of legal writing, these are common features of legal writing. You may also want to add some of your own points to check at the end. Give yourself time before submitting your writing to proofread your work.

		Have you checked?		**Done?**
1	The addressee and his/her/its address (if relevant)			
2	The tone of your work – have you adopted the correct level of professionalism and formality?			
3	Use of proper nouns (are these correct and consistent?)	Names of people (including judges)		
		Names of places		
		Names of organisations (e.g. law firms)		
		Names of courts		
		Case names		
4	Citations and other references			
5	Consistent use of defined terms	Are they defined?		
		Do they start with a capital letter?		
		Have you used the same term consistently?		
6	Use of complete sentences – read each sentence carefully – watch out for omitted words			
7	Correct use of punctuation	Apostrophes		
		Brackets (make sure there is an even number)		
		Quotation marks		
		Other punctuation		
8	Spelling – if you have one, refer to your list of words that you commonly mix up			
9	Consistent presentation of headings, numbered items, lists, bullet points			
10	Formatting and layout – does your work look professional and clearly laid out, and is the layout appropriate for the purpose and content?			

Chapter 6

Citations and Referencing

Chapter overview:

6.1 Referencing in legal writing
6.2 Adding footnotes to your legal writing
6.3 Citations – a detailed guide
6.4 Bibliography
6.5 Chapter summary

6.1 Referencing in legal writing

Referencing in legal writing provides the reader with information about the sources that you have used when researching your work. It creates an audit trail of your sources that should allow the reader to find not just your sources, but exactly where in the sources you have drawn your information, arguments or quotations from. As discussed in Chapter 3, sources can be primary sources (such as legislative provisions, cases and articles of the Constitution) or secondary sources (such as books, articles and reports).

In legal writing in Ireland and the United Kingdom, referencing of sources usually takes the form of citations in footnotes within the body of a document and a bibliography at the end of the document.[1] Footnotes and bibliographies should be sufficiently detailed that the reader can use the information provided to find the sources that you have used and to verify any statements, information or quotations that you have included in your document.

However, the extent to which complete and accurate referencing is necessary in your legal writing will depend on the purpose of a particular document. Footnotes and bibliographies are usually more relevant in academic writing, such as essays, dissertations, articles and books, or in the context of formal reports and research papers. More practical documents, such as letters of advice

---

[1] Some referencing styles require in-text citations, with a reference list at the end of the document. In-text citations involve including citation details in brackets within your text (rather than as footnotes). Other styles require endnotes rather than footnotes. Endnotes are structurally similar to footnotes, but they just appear at the end of the document, rather than at the bottom of each page. In-text citations and endnotes will not be discussed in detail in this book.

to clients, emails and internal memos do not necessarily need references. The recipient of these documents is more interested in the legal or practical advice being provided, rather than the background to that advice. Nevertheless, even in the context of documents that do not need to be referenced, it is always a good idea to keep your own list of the sources that you have consulted, just in case someone asks you to provide this information or you need to conduct further research.

If you are unsure whether a piece of legal writing needs to be referenced (and, if so, what format that referencing should take) consult your instructions or speak to the person who has assigned the piece of legal writing. The remainder of this chapter assumes that you are undertaking a piece of legal writing in which referencing is appropriate.

6.1.1 Plagiarism

Professional and academic integrity is important at third level and within a working environment. You should not (intentionally or inadvertently) pass someone else's work, ideas or arguments off as your own. As a result, if you quote, paraphrase, summarise or take an idea or argument from someone or somewhere else, you should consider whether an acknowledgment of this is necessary in a footnote. Failure to do this correctly, particularly in academic work, may be treated as plagiarism.

> **Practical Tip:**
>
> While plagiarism is most relevant with respect to the secondary sources that you rely on, you should also reference any primary sources that you rely on in order to make it clear to the reader where your information on the law has come from.

Your lecturers will often be able to identify something that is plagiarised simply by reading it – they may have read the relevant information somewhere else, they may be aware of whose idea or argument you are presenting as your own, or (something that happens surprisingly often) the plagiarised sentence or paragraph may be in a different font or different style to the rest of your work. Most third-level institutions now also require submission of assignments through plagiarism software, such as Turnitin. This software compares your work to that of other students, as well as to information on the internet, in books and in articles. To avoid a suggestion of plagiarism, you must be rigorous in your footnoting.

Practical Tip:

Particularly in an academic context, if you are in doubt as to whether or not to include a footnote, err on the side of caution and include it.

Plagiarism is defined in a similar way by third-level institutions across Ireland. Trinity College Dublin, for example, defines it as 'presenting the work or ideas of others as one's own without due acknowledgement',[2] University College Cork defines it as the 'presentation of work for credit without appropriate attribution',[3] Maynooth University defines it as an 'attempt to use an element of another person's work, without appropriate acknowledgement in order to gain academic credit'[4] and Waterford Institute of Technology provides that '[t]o plagiarise is when you use the ideas or words of another person without giving them explicit credit. Plagiarism therefore is passing off the work of others as one's own.'[5]

What is important to remember is that plagiarism does not require intention – you can plagiarise someone's work accidentally by forgetting to include a footnote or by not being meticulous in your referencing. Each of the following situations requires a footnote to avoid a suggestion of plagiarism.

Situation	Discussion
Direct quotations	Direct quotations must be included in quotation marks (single or double, make sure you use these consistently). Always footnote a direct quotation and include a pinpoint to exactly where in a source the relevant quotation is taken from.
Statements of fact	If you are making a factual statement and the information for this statement was taken from another source, you should footnote that source.

---

2 Trinity College Dublin, 'Plagiarism', Policy No: QPOLPlag (version 1, June 2016) <https://www.tcd.ie/teaching-learning/assets/pdf/PlagPolicy02-06-2016.pdf> accessed 6 November 2020 [6].
3 University College Cord, 'Plagiarism Policy' (version 2.0, May 2020) <https://www.ucc.ie/en/media/support/recordsandexaminations/documents/UCCPlagiarismPolicy-2020.pdf> accessed 6 November 2020 [1.1].
4 Maynooth University, 'Maynooth University Policy on Plagiarism' (version 2, September 2015) <https://www.maynoothuniversity.ie/sites/default/files/assets/document/MU%20Policy%20on%20Plagiarism%20Updated%20July%202019_0.pdf> accessed 6 November 2020, 1.
5 Waterford Institute of Technology 'Plagiarism', <https://www.wit.ie/images/uploads/Policies_PDF/WIT_anti-plagiarism_policy.pdf> accessed 6 November 2020 [1].

Situation	Discussion
Paraphrasing what someone else has said or written	A footnote is required not only when you quote someone, but also when you paraphrase what someone else has said or written by taking the substance of their statement and changing the words or phrasing used. Remember, paraphrasing is just rewriting someone else's work and must be footnoted.
Summarising what someone else has said or written	Like paraphrasing, summarising what someone else has said or written requires footnoting.
Presenting the substance of someone else's idea or argument (even if you write it in your own words)	During your research, you will come across different ideas and arguments. You may want to incorporate some of these in your own legal writing. However, if you take an idea or argument from someone else, you must acknowledge its source. Unless an idea or argument is your own, you should not present it as such.

Information that is common knowledge (for example, Dublin is the capital city of the Republic of Ireland) generally does not need to be footnoted. What constitutes 'common knowledge' is, unfortunately, a fluid concept. Consider whether the relevant piece of information is one that an educated reader is likely to know without having to look it up – for example, is it information that is widely known in society, information that is known within the context of a cultural or national group or information that is known to those in a particular field?[6] Ultimately, if you are unsure about whether information is or is not common knowledge, it is safest to include a footnote where you reference a source that confirms that information.

6.1.2 Referencing – do not leave it until the end

Keep notes of everything that you read during your research – you should make a note of the source's author, title, where it is available and any specific page, paragraph or section numbers that you need to pinpoint. Make sure that these details are complete and accurate as you will need them when you come to the writing stage of your legal writing. You will find it frustrating if you want to paraphrase a good legal argument, but you cannot remember who made the argument and you did not make any notes to indicate where the argument came from. It is, therefore, crucial that you develop a

---

[6] MIT, 'Academic Integrity at MIT – What is Common Knowledge?' <https://integrity.mit.edu/handbook/citing-your-sources/what-common-knowledge> accessed 6 November 2020.

system for linking your research notes to the various sources that you have consulted.

Similarly, when you start a piece of writing, get into the habit of adding footnotes and citation details as you go along – it is a much better use of your time to methodically footnote than to have to rush to find the citations for all of your footnotes as the submission deadline approaches. By not footnoting during the writing stage, you also increase the risk that you may forget to add a footnote to something that you have paraphrased or summarised. This could lead to a detection of plagiarism.

6.2 Adding footnotes to your legal writing

There are different styles for citing material referred to in legal writing. The first thing you must do when preparing any written work is to check whether you are required to follow a particular method of citation. Do this by checking the instructions that you have been given or the house style that you are required to follow.

If the guidance or house style specifies a particular method of citation, you should use that. For example, The Bluebook[7] is widely used in legal writing in the Unites States of America, OSCOLA[8] is used in the United Kingdom and OSCOLA Ireland[9] is used in Ireland. If you are not required to follow a specific citation style, choose one that is widely used. Apply this style consistently throughout your piece of legal writing.

---

[7] *The Bluebook: A Uniform System of Citation* < https://www.legalbluebook.com/> accessed 6 November 2020.

[8] OSCOLA (4th edn 2012) <https://www.law.ox.ac.uk/sites/files/oxlaw/oscola_4th_edn_hart_2012.pdf> accessed 6 November 2020.

[9] OSCOLA Ireland (2nd edn 2016) ('OSCOLA Ireland') and the related quick reference citation guide can be downloaded for free at: <http://legalcitation.ie/> accessed 6 November 2020.

Practical Tip:

Consistency and completeness are the most important characteristics of good legal citations. Make sure that you give the reader the information that he or she needs to find exactly where in a source you are referencing. Cite the same types of sources in the same way throughout your document and do not mix up or inconsistently apply citation styles. Be particularly careful if you copy a citation from another source – make sure that you conform to the citation style that you are using.

As part of your proofreading, pay attention to your footnotes – make sure that the information provided in these is accurate and that it is consistently presented.

You should also check whether footnotes (and bibliography) will be counted in any maximum word count to which you must adhere.

6.2.1 Inserting footnotes

When the footnote relates to a whole sentence, the footnote mark (that is, the number in superscript that links to the footnote at the end of the page) should generally go at the end (*not the beginning*) of the sentence, after the final punctuation for that sentence. If you are referencing a particular word, phrase or quotation *within* a sentence, the footnote mark should be included immediately after that reference, following any punctuation. However, if the word, phrase or quotation to which a footnote relates is in parentheses, the footnote mark should be included before the closing parenthesis.

Example:

Footnote mark at the end of a sentence: Lord Reid noted that it was never the law that acts of third parties always broke the chain of causation, but stated that the chain of causation will be broken unless that act of the third party is something 'very likely to happen'.[10]

Footnote mark within a sentence: The trial judge instructed the jury that the defendant was bound to act 'with such reasonable caution as a prudent man would have exercised'[11] under the circumstances.

---

[10] *Home Office v Dorset Yacht Co* [1970] AC 1004, 1028.
[11] *Vaughan v Menlove* 132 ER 490, 492.

> **Footnote of material in parentheses:** In the Supreme Court case of *Hayes v Minister for Finance*[12] (as cited again in the recent case of *McCarthy v James Kavanagh t/a Tekken Security*[13]) the Supreme Court cited with approval the following discussion of *novus actus interveniens*.

When you are typing your document using word processing software, you should use the software's footnote function to add footnotes. This will ensure that footnote numbers are automatically updated if you add or delete a footnote. Do not try to manually insert footnote marks and related footnotes.

- **To insert a footnote on Microsoft Word for Windows:** Place the cursor where you want the footnote mark to be added and press Ctrl + Alt + f. This will add the footnote mark in the text and a footnote in the document's footer. You will then add in the citation in the footnote.
- **To insert a footnote on a Mac (assuming you are using Word for Macs):** Place the cursor where you want the footnote mark to be added and press ⌘ + Option + f. You will then add in the citation as above.

When footnotes are added using your word processing software, footnote numbers should run sequentially (i.e. 1, 2, 3…). If you are preparing a longer document (for example, a PhD thesis) the footnote numbers will usually restart at 1 for each chapter.

Footnotes will typically be one to two font sizes smaller than the main text of your document, but they must be in the same font style as the main text. As a result, if your main text is Times New Roman, font-size 12, your footnotes will be Times New Roman, font-size 10.

6.2.2 Information in footnotes

The primary use of footnotes is to provide citation information for the sources that you have relied on, or referred to, in your legal writing. You can also include citation information for other related sources where the reader can find further details.

---

[12] [2007] 3 IR 190.
[13] [2018] IEHC 101.

Example:

As was noted in McMahon and Binchy, '[r]egard must be had to the object of the defendant's conduct. Where it has a high social utility, it will be regarded with more indulgence than where it has little or none.'[14]

———-

[14] McMahon and Binchy, *Law of Torts* (4th edn, Bloomsbury Professional 2013) [7.40]. See also, *McGarr v Dublin Bus/Bus Átha Cliath* [2016] IECA 366.

Quite often, you will find that authors include extra information in their footnotes. It is usually acceptable to include some information beyond pure citations in your footnotes (for example, a brief, related explanation that is interesting, but is not directly relevant to what you are discussing in the text). However, including extensive extra information or substantive arguments in footnotes should avoided. Some lecturers will refuse to read this information, particularly where it looks like a student is trying to circumvent a word limit by including everything beyond that limit in the footnotes. Similarly, some academic publishers prohibit anything beyond citations and simple explanations in footnotes. As a result, if you are making arguments or statements in your footnotes that are key to the substance of what you are writing, these should be moved to the body of your text.

6.2.3 Pinpoints in footnotes

The purpose of footnotes is to give the reader the information needed to find any of the sources that you cite. Where you refer to a specific page, paragraph or section number within a source, the related footnote should include a pinpoint reference to that exact page, paragraph or section number. Remember, many sources are long, and it may not be helpful to the reader if you just point them to the source generally. This is particularly the case for quotations – if you include a quotation from page 380 of a 400-page book, a footnote that refers to the book generally without pinpointing the page where the quotation came from will not really assist the reader in trying to find that quotation.

As a result, unless you are referring to a source as a general authority for a point of law, or as a source of information generally, always give a pinpoint reference.

> **Practical Tip:**
>
> As a general rule, any time you quote from, summarise or paraphrase the text of, a source you should: (1) cite that source; *and* (2) pinpoint the place in the source to which your citation is referring.

6.2.4 Punctuation in footnotes

The citation in footnotes should start with a capital letter and should end with a full stop (or other end punctuation, such as an exclamation or question mark if appropriate). If there is more than one citation in a single footnote, separate them with a semi-colon.

> **Example:**
>
> The acts of the third party must be highly foreseeable.[15]
>
> ———-
>
> [15] *Cunningham v McGrath Brothers* [1964] IR 209; *Home Office* v *Dorset Yacht Co* [1970] AC 1004, 1028.

Use of other punctuation within the text of the footnote will be driven by the citation style that you are using – for example, OSCOLA Ireland discourages use of full stops in footnotes, other than at the end of sentences. Abbreviations, acronyms or initials in footnotes should not, therefore, be followed by a full stop if you are following OSCOLA Ireland.

6.2.5 References within the footnotes of your sources

The sources that you use in your legal research (particularly secondary sources) may themselves rely on other sources for information, ideas and arguments. A textbook may, for example, quote a judge from a case, or may paraphrase an argument from another academic. In each case, the source that you are reading should include a footnote in which it cites the relevant underlying source that the author has relied on. This raises the question as to which source you should cite in your own legal writing.

Ideally, you should try to find the underlying source that is being cited in the footnote and read it. This is particularly important where the underlying source is a primary source of law, such as cases and legislation. You can then cite the underlying source in your own footnote. Finding the underlying source is important as it allows you to make sure the information was quoted, paraphrased or summarised correctly and that the citation provided is correct. It is not uncommon to find that material from an underlying source has been misquoted, presented out of context or incorrectly cited. If you do not find and read that underlying source, and instead rely only on someone else's footnote, you risk making the same mistake.

It is not, however, always possible to find the underlying source. In such cases, you should cite the underlying source using the footnote in the source that you are reading. You should then acknowledge that you have not read the underlying source by noting 'as quoted/cited in [*citation for the source you are reading*].'

> **Example:**
>
> As one commentator noted:
>> ... causation is no more than the connection deemed necessary in tort law between, on one hand, a defendant's misconduct, that of a person for whom the defendant is responsible, or the existence of a source of danger, and on the other, compensable damage.[16]
>
> ----
>
> [16] Christian von Bar, *The Common European Law of Torts* (2nd vol, Oxford University Press 2000), note 440, as quoted in Cees van Dam, *European Tort Law* (Oxford University Press 2007), 1100.

6.2.6 Cross-referencing and Latin terms in footnotes

Typically, if you have included a citation in full in one footnote, subsequent references to the same source can simply cross-refer to the earlier footnote. Do make sure, however, that you also include any pinpoint reference that is relevant to the subsequent footnote (for example, if your citation is to a different page of a book that you have already cited, you would cross-refer to the earlier footnote and include the relevant page number).

How you cross-refer to earlier footnotes will be determined by the citation style that you are using. Some citations styles require you to use Latin directions (discussed below), while others discourage this. OSCOLA Ireland, for example recommends the following.
- You avoid using Latin directions other than 'ibid'. The Latin abbreviation 'ibid' means 'in the same place' and should only be used (unitalicised) if you cross-refer to the citation used in the *immediately preceding* footnote. Remember to add in a new pinpoint reference if you are referring to a different page, paragraph or section number of the same source. If there is more than one

citation in the preceding footnote, use ibid only if you are referring to all of the citations included in the preceding footnote.

- For cross-references to footnotes other than those immediately above, you identify the source (for example, by including the author's name), followed in brackets by 'n' and the footnote number to which you are cross-referring, and finally any relevant pinpoint reference.

Example:

[17] McMahon, Bryan and Binchy, William, *Law of Torts* (4th edn, Bloomsbury Professional, 2013) 62.
[18] *Cunningham v McGrath Brothers* [1964] IR 209; *Home Office v Dorset Yacht Co* [1970] AC 1004, 1028.
[19] McMahon and Binchy (n 17) 80.
[20] *Cunningham v McGrath Brothers* (n 18) 211.
[21] ibid, 213.

If the citation style that you are using requires use of Latin directions, set out below are some commonly used abbreviations for these directions. Remember, the below are *not* OSCOLA Ireland-compliant.

Latin directions	Meaning	Use	Example
supra	above	This can be used to direct the reader to an earlier footnote.	[22] This case is discussed in detail *supra* note 7. [23] *Cunningham v McGrath Brothers, supra* note 18.
infra	below	This can be used to direct the reader to a later footnote.	[24] *Glasgow Corporation v Muir, infra* note 32.
op. cit.	the work cited	This alerts the reader that the full citation of the source is set out in an earlier footnote. Always identify the source before adding *op. cit.* Include the relevant pinpoint reference.	[25] Fleming, John G, *The Law of Torts* (9th edn, Sweet & Maxwell 1998), 130. [26] *McComisky v McDermott* [1974] IR 75, 89. [27] Fleming, *op. cit.*, 145.

Whatever approach to cross-referencing you use, it is always a good idea to include any reference to another footnote number as an automatic cross-reference. This will ensure that if your footnote numbers change (for example, if you add in a new footnote), the cross-references within your document will all update to reflect this.

- **To insert a cross-reference on Microsoft Word for Windows and on a Mac (assuming you are using Word**

for Macs): Place the cursor where you want to include the cross-reference (e.g. after the 'n' or 'note'). In the ribbon at the top of your screen click 'Insert' and then 'Cross-reference'. This will cause a dialog box to pop up. In the 'Reference type' drop-down menu, select 'Footnote' and in the 'Insert reference to' drop-down menu, select 'Footnote number'. This will bring up all the footnotes in your document. Find the footnote that you want to cross-reference to and click 'insert'.

- **To update all the cross-references on Microsoft Word for Windows:** Highlight the footnotes in your document, press Fn + F9.
- **To update all the cross-references on a Mac (assuming you are using Word for Macs):** Highlight the footnotes in your document, press ⌘ + A + F9.

> **Practical Tip:**
>
> As part of your final proofread of your document, do a word search for 'Error!' to flag up any automatic cross-references that are broken. This happens when the underlying footnote to which the cross-reference relates has been deleted.

6.3 Citations – a quick guide

Should referencing of authorities be relevant to your piece of legal writing, it is important that any citations and references included are complete, accurate and helpful. Remember, the citations and references that you include must provide enough detail to allow the reader to find the relevant authority with ease. The reader should also be able to use your citations to find any specific quotations that you have included, or passages that you have paraphrased, from an authority. To help with the referencing process, make a note of complete citations of authorities as you conduct your research.

The section below provides tips that you may find helpful as you cite more commonly used material in your legal writing. You should always obtain a copy of, and familiarise yourself with, any applicable citation style guide that you are using.[14]

---

[14] Such as OSCOLA Ireland. The section below will include references to the applicable sections of OSCOLA Ireland, so that you can refer to these as you write.

6.3.1 Primary sources

(1) EU law:[15]

- For Regulations and Directives, ensure that you include the type of legislation at the beginning of the citation (for example: Regulation (EU) 2017/1129 of the European Parliament and of the Council of 14 June 2017 on the prospectus to be published when securities are offered to the public or admitted to trading on a regulated market, and repealing Directive 2003/71/EC).
- Always check the Official Journal of the European Union (OJ)[16] for the full reference details of EU legislation.

(2) Irish Constitution:[17]

- If it is not obvious from the text, consider including reference to 'of the Constitution' in the citation.
- Capitalise the 'A' when you are referring to one or more specific articles within the Constitution.
- If, however, you are just referring to 'articles of the Constitution' more generically, the 'a' should be lowercase.
- Pinpoint references to articles of the Constitution should include the main Article number, the section number and the sub-section number. Follow the sub-section number with a degree symbol (for example: Article 9.2.1°).

(3) Primary legislation (Acts of the Oireachtas):[18]

- Cite primary legislation by its short title and year.
- Section 1 of an Act of the Oireachtas will generally provide the short title for that piece of legislation.
- Check the relevant citation style guide to confirm whether there should be a full stop between the 's' (meaning section), 'sch' (meaning schedule) or 'pt' (meaning part) and the number.
- If you are referring to multiple section numbers include 'ss' and then the section numbers (for example: Companies Act 2014, ss 281–282).

(4) Secondary legislation (Statutory Instruments):[19]

- Cite secondary legislation by its title, year and its statutory instrument number (for example: Companies

---

[15] OSCOLA Ireland, section 2.5.
[16] Official Journal of the European Union, <https://eur-lex.europa.eu/oj/direct-access.html> accessed 6 November 2020.
[17] OSCOLA Ireland, section 2.1.
[18] OSCOLA Ireland, section 2.3.
[19] OSCOLA Ireland, section 2.4.

(Accounting) Act 2017 (Commencement) Order 2017, SI 2017/246, art 4).
- Regulation 1 of a Statutory Instrument will generally provide the title by which it is to be cited.
- Check the relevant citation style guide to confirm whether there should be a full stop between the 'reg' (meaning regulation), 'r' (meaning rule) or 'art' (meaning article) and the number.
- If you are referring to multiple rule numbers – include 'rr' and then the rule numbers.

(5) Irish case law:[20]
- The 'v' between party names should be lowercase. Check the relevant citation style guide to confirm whether there should be a full stop after the 'v'.
- There are a number of case reporting systems that are relevant to Irish cases.
  - A citation is a 'neutral' citation if it does not refer to a particular series of law reports. Instead, neutral citations identify the year of the judgment, the court where the case was heard and the case number. The case number is a sequential number in the relevant court for that year, so the citation '[2020] IESC 2' refers to the second judgment issued by the Irish Supreme Court in 2020.
  - Newer cases may only have a neutral citation. For example: *McGarr v Dublin Bus/Bus Átha Cliath* [2016] IECA 366 [4] (Peart J).
  - Older cases may not have a neutral citation and instead are unreported or reported in one of the law reports (such as the Irish Reports or the Irish Law Reports Monthly). For example: *Breslin v Corcoran* [2003] 2 IR 203 (SC) 206 (Fennelly J).
  - Where a case is reported in a law report series, the citation takes the format of identifying the year it was printed in the law report (this may be in the calendar year following the judgment, if the judgment was issued in the later months of a year), followed by the law report series number, the law report acronym and the first page on which the judgment is printed.
  - Some cases have both types of citation (in which case, you should cite both and separate them with a comma). For example: *Simpson v Governor*

---

[20] OSCOLA Ireland, section 2.2.

of Mountjoy Prison, Irish Prison Service, Minister for Justice and Equality, Ireland and the Attorney General [2019] IESC 81 [1], [2020] 1 ILRM 81 [1] (MacMenamin J).

- Check the relevant citation style guide to confirm whether there should be a full stop in the acronym of law reports.
- There are no official law reports in Ireland (although the Irish Reports and the Irish Law Reports Monthly are regarded as the most authoritative reports).
- Remember to include a pinpoint reference if you are quoting from, paraphrasing, or just referring to a specific section of, a case.
    o If a judgment has numbered paragraphs, your pinpoint should refer to a specific paragraph.
    o If a judgment has no paragraph numbers, but does have page numbers, your pinpoint should refer to a specific page.
    o Check the relevant citation style guide to confirm how paragraphs or pages should be pinpointed and whether they are introduced with the abbreviations 'para' or 'p'. Some citation styles identify pinpoint references to paragraphs by putting the paragraph numbers in square brackets.
- If a judgment has no paragraph or page numbers, do not include a pinpoint.
- If you are quoting from a judgment, identify the judge who delivered the judgment as follows: 'pinpoint *(surname of judge that you are quoting* CJ/J/P)'.

(6) Judgments of the European Court of Justice (ECJ) and General Court (GC):[21]

- The European courts have recently updated their cataloguing system. As a result, every existing case has now been given a European Case Law Identifier (ECLI) number and every future case will only be given an ECLI number and published electronically.
- Case numbers for cases after 1989 are given the prefix 'C-' (for ECJ cases) or 'T-' (for GC cases).
- Where a case is reported in the official reports, use this as your citation: ECR I for ECJ cases; ECR II for GC cases.
- For reported cases with both an ECR reference and an ECLI number, check with your lecturer or the relevant

---

[21] OSCOLA Ireland, section 2.5.2 (although please note that this section is slightly out of date with the introduction of the ECLI system).

citation style guide to confirm whether details of both should be included or just the ECLI number.
- If no report is available, just refer to the ECLI number.
- Be careful when you download material relating to ECJ and GC cases as Advocate General Opinions will have their own separate ECLI number, which will be different to the main judgment's ECLI number.

(7) **Foreign cases:**[22]
- Cite a foreign case in the same way that it is cited in its home jurisdiction (although remove any full stops used in abbreviations in the original citation if not permitted by the citation style that you are following).
- For English cases, you may find it helpful to refer to the OSCOLA method of citation.[23]
- Judgments from English courts may be published in multiple law reports – the Law Reports series is regarded as the most authoritative and should be the law report cited, if available.
- If a case has not been reported in the Law Reports, the Weekly Law Reports or the All England Law Reports version can be cited.

6.3.2 Secondary sources[24]

(1) **Books and edited collections:**
- Carefully check the relevant citation style guide for details about how to cite the names of a book's author(s) or editor(s) – these requirements can vary significantly between citation styles.
- If a book has more than three authors, include the name of the first author and then the words 'and others' or '*et al.*' depending on the citation style that you are using. You will include full author details in your bibliography.
- A book will have a new edition when it is updated and reprinted. If the book that you are citing has multiple editions, it is important that you cite the correct edition – this information is typically included at the front of a book, prior to the table of contents.
- An edited collection is a book where each chapter is written by a different author. One or more editors will

---

[22] OSCOLA Ireland, section 1.4
[23] OSCOLA, n 8. More information about OSCOLA can be found on the University of Oxford, Faculty of Law, 'OSCOLA' website: <www.law.ox.ac.uk/research-subject-groups/publications/oscola> accessed 6 November 2020.
[24] OSCOLA Ireland, section 3.

be in charge of reviewing the chapters and ensuring that they fit within the wider book project. For edited collections it is particularly important that you make a note of the name of the editor(s) and the name of the author of any individual chapter that you are referencing.

(2) Journal articles:

- While many academic journals are still published in hard copy, not all libraries hold hard copies of journals. Instead, many university and other third-level institution's libraries now subscribe to electronic versions of journals through online legal databases, such as Westlaw IE. You must cite a journal article that you have downloaded from a database as if you were reading that journal article in hard copy. As a result, you should *not* include reference to the online database that you used, the online link to the article or the date that you downloaded the article. You must treat the journal article like a hard copy source.

- Carefully check the relevant citation style guide for details about how to cite the names of a journal article's author(s) – as is the case for book authors, these requirements can vary significantly between citation styles.

- Ensure that your citation includes both the first page of the article *and* a pinpoint reference to the relevant page of the article that is relevant. For example: Gemma Turton and Sally Kyd 'Causing controversy: interpreting the requirements of causation in criminal law and tort law' (2019) 70(4) NILQ 425 [*this is the first page of the article*], 430 [*this is the pinpoint reference*].

(3) Internet sources:

- Material taken from an internet source must be cited. How it is cited will depend on how much information you are provided with. What is key is that the reader should be able to find the relevant source based on the information that you include in your footnote.

- If the material is also available in hard copy, you will generally cite just the hard copy version (rather than including reference to the website or webpage where you accessed the material).

- Where the relevant source is only available online (for example, a website or online publication), then you must include the webpage's URL.

- Include the author's name if available. If the particular

webpage that you are citing has no author details listed, just start your citation with the title of the webpage.

- Citation styles generally also require that you include the date on which you last accessed each webpage. This reflects the reality that webpages are frequently updated or removed. Material that may have been available at the time you were undertaking your legal writing may not be available by the time that writing is being read. By including the date that you last accessed that information, you make it clear that the relevant information was available at a particular date.
- It is a good idea to revisit all websites included in your legal writing just before it is submitted or sent. When you do so, update the 'last accessed' date. This will ensure that: (1) all of these last accessed dates are the same; and (2) you are providing the reader with the most up to date information that you can.
- Remove hyperlinks that are automatically created when you type in a URL in most word processing programs.

6.4 Bibliography

A bibliography is not always required in legal writing (for example, not all academic journals include a bibliography at the end of articles). Bibliographies are more common in longer pieces of legal writing, such as essays and dissertations. Check your instructions to confirm whether you should also be preparing a bibliography.

A bibliography is a list at the end of a document that sets out, in alphabetical order, all of the *secondary* sources referred to in the document. You do not need to include cases, legislation or articles of the Constitution in bibliographies. Your bibliography helps the reader to quickly find and scan a list of the secondary sources that you have used in preparing your document.

> **Practical Tip:**
>
> When creating a bibliography, students often simply copy and paste their footnotes into a bibliography, and then alphabetise these. This results in the same source being referred to multiple times in the bibliography with different pinpoint references. This is incorrect. Remember, each source only needs to be referred to once in the bibliography.

The format of references in bibliographies is similar to footnotes except the following.

- Bibliographies should not include pinpoint references and, even if you refer to a source multiple times in your document, that source only needs to be referred to once in your bibliography.
- The author's surname usually comes first, followed by the author's forenames as initials (no comma between surname and initials).
- Sources with no author should start with a double em-dash (——) in place of the author's name.
- There is no full stop at the end of references in a bibliography.

> **Example:**
>
> Footnote: Bryan M E McMahon and William Binchy, *Law of Torts* (4th edn, Bloomsbury Professional 2013) 58.
>
> Bibliography: McMahon B M E and Binchy W, *Law of Torts* (4th edn, Bloomsbury Professional 2013)

6.5 Chapter summary

- Clear and accurate references in the form of footnotes, endnotes or in-text citations are important to ensure that you do not plagiarise someone else's work and make it clear where your information or ideas have come from.

- Plagiarism does not require intent – it can happen inadvertently if you do not reference rigorously.

- Follow the citation style required by your instructions or house style. If no guidance on this is provided, pick a citation style that is commonly used and apply it consistently throughout your document.

- Always include as much information in your footnotes as is needed for the reader to find the sources that you have referenced.

- Confirm whether you also need to include a bibliography in your legal writing.

Part III
Legal Research and Writing in Specific Situations

Legal Research and Writing in Specific Situations

Chapter 7 draws together the skills and techniques discussed in the other chapters of this book and applies them to specific legal writing situations that you may face. This chapter provides you with tips and guidance for a variety of situations, from essays to emails to letters. In each of these situations, principles of good legal research and writing will be relevant. However, different types of documents raise different considerations. This chapter outlines some of these considerations and provides you with practical guidance to help you to produce written work that is appropriate for the situation.

While the sections of this chapter should be read in conjunction with earlier chapters, they can be consulted on a section by section basis as you are faced with new writing tasks.

Please bear in mind that the information provided in this chapter is guidance only – any style of writing, formatting or presentation preferred (or demanded) by your lecturer, employer or client should be followed in preference to the guidance below.

7.1 Written assignments – essay and problem questions

Written assignments in law can take a variety of forms, the most common being those based on essay-style questions and those based on problem-style questions. Both essay and problem questions demand thorough research, an accurate understanding of the law, and clear and appropriate presentation. However, how you approach and structure your answers to essay and problem questions will differ. Always bear in mind the style of question that you are dealing with when preparing an answer to your written assignment.

7.1.1 General tips for written assignments

A. Read the question and consider what it is asking you to do

A good written assignment answers the question asked. This tip seems obvious, but is so often not followed in full (or at all) by students in written assignment answers. Take the time to read the question thoroughly several times. Underline important statements and directions (for essay questions), and key facts and who you are advising (for problem questions). As you read the question, think carefully about what you are being asked to do – identify the specific task that you have been set. Failure to do this early on could result in you conducting research that is not relevant, including a discussion of the law that is too general or getting side-tracked as you write.

If you give the text of the question only a cursory read before you start researching and writing, you may misunderstand what you are being asked to do, you may misinterpret the facts, or you may overlook a crucial detail.

B. Support what you are saying with authority

Written assignments in law are designed to test your understanding of the law. It is, therefore, essential that when you state a legal principle, you provide a citation to the source of that legal principle. You should also include a full citation, with pinpoint reference, every time you quote from, paraphrase or take an idea from another source.

Add citations to your written assignment as you go along. Do not leave it until you have written your assignment in full to retrospectively add in citation details. If your written assignment instructions ask for a bibliography, ensure that you build this up throughout the research and writing phases of your written assignment. See Chapter 6 for further details on citations and bibliographies.

C. Manage your time

Completing a written assignment can be a time-consuming exercise. It requires you to conduct detailed research, to analyse a legal principle or to apply that principle to a set of facts, to structure your writing in a way that is clear, logical and polished, and to proofread your work before submitting it.

You should not, therefore, leave your written assignment until the last minute to complete. Treat each written assignment as an opportunity to develop valuable time management skills. In doing so, you should create a plan for your research in which you allocate an amount of time to each portion of your written assignment (do not forget to build in time at the end for proofreading). You will need to be flexible with this plan, but if you try to anticipate how long you will dedicate to research, writing and polishing your work, you can balance this with other demands on your time.

7.1.2 Essay-style questions

Assignments framed as essay-style questions will typically involve a quotation, statement or reference to a legal topic that you are asked to discuss, analyse or evaluate. This is an opportunity for you to demonstrate that you understand the legal principles underpinning the topic of the essay. In an essay-style question you will typically be given less guidance in terms of structure than you would for a problem-style question. However, it is unlikely that you will be asked to simply set out all the law that you know on a topic. It is, therefore, vital that you read and understand what you are being asked to do and that you take time to plan the structure of your essay.

A. *Understanding the essay brief*

Chapter 2 of this book discussed how to plan your research. In particular, it considered how you should identify the research question(s) to answer from the essay brief that you have been given. However, when you look at a brief for the first time there are other, more general things that you should be thinking about. These things will help you to provide an appropriate essay-style response to the assignment.

The first thing to look for is the form of the question itself. The question may be formed as:
- one or two simple sentences that you must respond or react to;
- a quotation from a legal source plus an instruction on how to respond to that quotation;
- a direct question; or
- a statement.

Whatever the form of the question, take a moment to consider *what* you are being asked to do in the essay. If you are presented with a direct question, make sure that your essay answers *that* question. If you are given a quotation, then make sure that your answer is directly relevant to the issues raised by *that* quotation.

The second thing to consider carefully is the instructions that you are given about *how* you should approach the question. Identify any 'instruction verbs' in the question.

Instruction Verb	Explanation
Analyse	The question wants you to break the topic into logical parts and to methodically examine these supported by relevant arguments from primary and secondary sources. Explain why and how the legal facts that you know are relevant to the relevant legal issue. This is not just a narrative description of the topic generally; you should reach a conclusion as to your position with respect to the topic.
Contrast	The question wants you to consider two or more different positions and to draw out the differences and similarities between them. Do not simply describe each position – consider how and why they differ or are similar.
Describe	The question wants you to explain the topic in detail and to provide a thorough discussion of this. Ensure that you include reference to primary and secondary source material.
Discuss	When you are asked to 'discuss' something, you should examine the topic in detail and delve into the implications of what you have discussed. Examine relevant arguments and shortcomings.
Evaluate	The question wants you to consider the merit or truth about one or more things – you will need to come to a conclusion on this. So, weigh up two or more different plausible solutions to a legal issue and explain which one you believe should be preferred, and why.
Examine	This is similar to questions that ask you to 'describe' something, although it is advisable to adopt a critical stance here and to highlight benefits and shortcomings.
Synthesise	When looking at a legal issue, take two or more legal concepts that may be unrelated to the issue or to each other, and create a solution to the legal issue by putting them together.

The purpose of giving you an essay-based assignment is to see how well you can think about the issues and problems that are raised within a particular legal field, and how well you can articulate and defend your opinion on these issues and problems. Therefore, even if you are not explicitly instructed to respond 'critically' or 'evaluatively' in an assignment, you should assume (unless the instructions are to survey or outline the law only) that your task is nonetheless to provide some critical commentary on the legal issues raised by the assignment.

The difference between critically analysing and evaluating the law, as opposed to just giving a narrative overview of all of the law on the topic, could be the difference between lower second/third class grades and upper second/first class grades.[1] If you simply set out what the law says, when you should be critically analysing and evaluating it, you will not be awarded the highest grades. Knowing what the law says, and being able to comprehend and then describe it, are relatively easy skills to master – your lecturers want to know that you have these skills, but they are also looking for more.[2] Being able to analyse, synthesise and evaluate the law are harder skills – these are the skills that your lecturers want to see you demonstrate in an essay.[3]

> **Practical Tip:**
>
> Chapter 1 of this book noted that learning legal skills is a gradual process that involves regular practice. Becoming skilled in legal analysis, synthesis and evaluation is perhaps the perfect case study for this. You are not expected to pick up these skills instantly. Rather, you will develop them gradually by paying close attention to the feedback you receive on your legal writing, and implementing the feedback in the next essay that you write. Embrace this reality – commit to trying your best to analyse, synthesise and evaluate when you answer an essay question.

B. Structuring your answer

(i) The overall structure of your essay

The order in which you present your ideas to the reader in an

---

[1] Critical thinking, and how it is assessed in law assignments, is discussed in: Nick James and Kelley Burton, 'Measuring the Critical Thinking Skills of Law Students Using a Whole-of-Curriculum Approach' (2017) 27 Legal Education Review 1.

[2] For more details, see Paul Callister, 'Time to Blossom: An Inquiry into Bloom's Taxonomy as a Hierarchy and Means for Teaching Legal Research Skills' (2010) 102(2) Law Library Journal 191.

[3] These skills are discussed at greater length in: Nelson P Miller and Bradley J Charles, 'Meeting the Carnegie Report's Challenge to Make Legal Analysis Explicit—Subsidiary Skills to the IRAC Framework' (2009) 59(2) Journal of Legal Education 192.

essay is important. The most accurate and detailed analysis will still not persuade the reader if that reader cannot follow the flow of the points being made. To persuade the reader, you need to introduce concepts in an order that makes it clear how the evidence fits together and supports the main argument(s) you are trying to make. That is why it is key that you adopt a strong and clear structure in your essays.

Map out a provisional structure for your essay when you plan your argument (as discussed in Chapter 2), although be conscious that when you start writing you may find that you need to change this structure. This is perfectly acceptable. The structure of your argument must adapt as the argument itself develops over the course of your research and writing. The graphic below illustrates what a well-structured argument should look like.

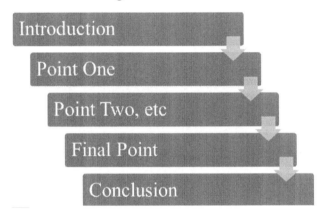

(1) **Introduction:** Start with your introduction – this must set out the main argument(s) that you will make, any contextual information that is necessary for the reader to understand why you are making this argument and how it fits within the relevant legal field. Your introduction should also set out the structure of how your argument will be developed.

(2) **Points within your essay:** After the introduction, you must start with the point that naturally and logically must be made before all others, in order for your overall argument to make sense. Your second point must be the one that naturally and logically must follow in order for your argument to continue to make sense. It should both require the first point to have been made in order to make sense and require further points to be made in order for the overall argument to make sense. Continue until you have reached the final point that you want to make. This final point should rely on all other points

having been made in order for it to make sense, and by this stage you should not need to say anything further for your overall argument to make sense.

Sometimes you may have points in the middle of your structure that could be made in any order, while still allowing your argument to flow logically. If this is the case, place the point which is most detailed and for which you have the strongest evidence first. Alternatively, if those points have a chronological element to them, arrange them according to this chronology.

(3) **Conclusion:** Your conclusion should summarise the arguments you have made, and the steps you have gone through in order to make them. You should not say anything new in your conclusion – any new points of substance will only lead the reader to wonder why they have not been developed in more detail in the body of your essay.

When devising your structure, keep in mind that a strong structure will move your argument along and will add something new at each stage (other than the conclusion). Consider the following things.

- Think about how each point will progress the overall argument you are trying to make. This is also important because organising your points logically is only half of the job – the other half is making this structure clear to your reader. As you finish each point, tell the reader where you are in your overall argument, what the point has added to this argument and what you will add with the point that you are about to make.

- Use headings to divide up the main parts of your essay. You should also use sub-headings to define the major stages of your argument. You do not need to place a sub-heading before each point that you make – this will just make your essay look cluttered and overly complicated. You should group your points into clear stages (you might only have one, more complex point in a stage, or you may have two or three more simple points). Provide a sub-heading for each stage. This breaks the essay up visually, making it easier to follow. It also helps the reader to identify the main points of progression of your argument.

- Clear transitions between each section of your essay, as well as between individual points, are important. In general, clear signposting within your essay allows the reader to take stock of how your argument is developing, the key constituent elements of that argument and how they relate to each other.

(ii) Structure within points

The importance of having a strong and clear structure does not just refer to structure between points. It also refers to structure within points. The graphic below illustrates what you should try to do within each paragraph, or set of paragraphs, that develop a point of your argument.

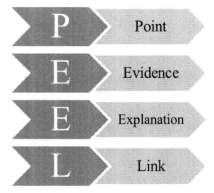

- First: Clearly set out the **Point** that you are making.
- Second: Provide the **Evidence** that supports your point.
- Third: **Explain** how the evidence that you have provided backs up the point that you are making. There can be a certain amount of intertwining of evidence and explanation, but in general you should present a piece of evidence before you explain its relevance to your point.
- Finally: **Link** the point that you have made back to your overall argument, making it clear to the reader how the point advances that overall argument.

In essays, the third and fourth stages of the 'PEEL' (point, evidence, explanation, link) structure are frequently omitted. A student may make a point and provide evidence for the point, but then not provide any explanation as to how the evidence supports the point, or any link back to the main argument. Remember, a law essay will generally require more than just a discussion of the law – you need to engage with the relevant legal principles and evidence and tie these back to what the essay wants you to do. As a general rule, if you are consistently and satisfactorily completing the third and fourth stages of the 'PEEL' structure, then you are doing the type of work that is required to demonstrate and develop the harder skills of analysis, synthesis and evaluation discussed above.

7.1.3 Problem-style questions

As well as more traditional essay-style questions, you may also face a situation where you are asked to prepare a written assignment based on a problem question. In this situation, you will be presented with a set of facts and be asked to advise one or more parties. This replicates a situation that you may face in legal practice, where a client presents you with a series of facts and asks for your advice on their legal position.

A. Read the question

Do not read a problem question quickly, conclude that it deals with (for example) causation, and then write everything that you know about causation. Problem questions require you to respond to the facts with which you are presented. You must, therefore:

- apply the law to the facts that you are given;
- provide legal advice to the correct party; and
- reach a conclusion as to the party's legal position and any relevant legal liability – you should not leave your answer to a problem question open-ended.

Read the facts of the problem question and make sure that you understand these. Underline relevant facts, keep a list of the parties and their respective role in the set of facts, create your own timeline of the facts to help you to organise and understand them.

Refer back to the facts as you research and write your answer. This is because facts that you had previously thought were irrelevant may become relevant as you conduct more detailed research and facts that you had thought were crucial may become less so in light of your research. Remember, a problem question requires you to do more than just explain the law; you must apply the law to the facts and provide your 'client' with clear and relevant advice.

B. Using a framework

A problem question assignment is designed to teach you how to apply the law in real life situations. Doing this effectively requires you to be disciplined and structured in your thinking and writing. For this reason, numerous 'frameworks' have been created to summarise the process that should be used to tackle a problem question.[4]

The most common of these is the 'IRAC' framework (this is also referred to as 'ILAC'). Under this framework, you should:

- consider the legal **I**ssues raised by the facts of the problem question;
- identify the legal **R**ule(s) (or **L**aw(s) if using the ILAC framework) that are relevant to these issues,
- **A**pply these rules to resolve the issues in light of the legal principles; and
- reach a **C**onclusion in which you state what the outcome will be for whomever it is you have been instructed to advise.

This section uses the IRAC framework to demonstrate how problem question frameworks can help you to answer problem questions. Much of the advice below is also relevant if you prefer to use another framework.

There are three reasons why using a framework is helpful when answering a problem question.

- Using a framework will help you to structure your thinking, so that you do not forget to include important issues. It helps you to consider how best to address those important issues and, in doing so, to produce an analytically sound and satisfactory answer.
- Using a framework will help you to organise your writing so that you are communicating your analysis in a way that will be clear for the reader.
- Using a framework in the early stages of your law degree will help you build competence in legal reasoning, so that when you are faced with scenarios that are more complex

---

[4] The teaching of problem question frameworks has been criticised by some as over-simplifying the complexity of legal analysis, for example: Laura P Graham, 'Why-Rac? Revisiting the Traditional Paradigm for Writing About Legal Analysis' (2015) 63 Kansas Law Review 681. However, others have defended the teaching of problem question frameworks on the basis that they encourage students to see the value of thinking about legal problems in a structured way, and provide students with a starting point from which to think and develop the skills involved in writing effective legal analysis, for example: Kelley Burton, '"Think Like a Lawyer" Using a Legal Reasoning Grid and Criterion-Referenced Assessment Rubric on IRAC (Issue, Rule, Application, Conclusion)' (2017) 10(2) Journal of Learning Design 57; Nelson P Miller and Bradley J Charles, 'Meeting the Carnegie Report's Challenge to Make Legal Analysis Explicit—Subsidiary Skills to the IRAC Framework' (2009) 59(2) Journal of Legal Education 192.

or unusual, you have built the necessary analytical skills to allow you to identify the necessary legal solutions.

C. IRAC in practice

The following table summarises the things you should be considering when you use the IRAC framework, in order for it to be a useful aid to answering problem questions.

Issue	• Read the facts of the problem question very carefully. Before you do anything else, you must work out what is going on. Who are the parties? What have they done and which of their actions are material to the problem? • Do not make up or infer any facts that are not stated in the question. You can only work with the facts that you have been given, just like in real life. • There could be several important legal issues – some obvious, some not – look carefully at the facts for both the obvious and not so obvious issues. Underline the issues that you identify. • Many of the facts will be relevant to addressing the legal issues you have identified, but not necessarily *every* fact. Look carefully at the facts and decide which are relevant to the legal issues you have identified, and which are not.
Rule	• What *current* law is *relevant* to the facts and the legal issues? What general legal principle or rule of law can we identify from the different legal sources? You should be looking to identify a rule that will allow you to determine the legal consequences that arise from the stated facts. • It is likely that you will need to find more than one rule in each problem question. There should be at least one for each legal issue that you identified at stage 1. • Some rules might be well-known, easy to identify and perhaps will come from only one legal authority (like one case or one statute). Some rules might be more obscure and difficult to identify. You may need to extract relevant ideas and principles from several cases, statutes and other sources, and then combine them to build the appropriate rule. Try to be aware of the type of rule you are dealing with and put in the required effort depending on how easy that rule is to identify.
	• Try to explain how you have identified the legal rules that you will apply to the facts – which sources did you draw them from and why? • If there are plausible alternative interpretations of what the relevant rule is, be able to explain why you have rejected these alternatives.

Application	• Which order should the legal issues that you have identified be addressed in? The answer to some of the legal issues raised by a problem question may depend on the answer to other legal issues. Start with the issue that must logically be addressed first.
	• Try to avoid rendering your analysis on certain points useless by discussing hypotheticals that you then make redundant with later points. There is no point analysing at length how one rule would apply, only to say in the next paragraph 'but actually, the application of this next rule means that everything that I have just said will not actually happen.'
	• Are the requirements of the rules satisfied by the facts? If so, why? Use analogies to, and distinctions from, previous legal precedent to illustrate and explain.
	• If there is any ambiguity in whether the rule is satisfied, what is your opinion on how that ambiguity should be resolved? This is where you could use academic authority to help you to explain your opinion. Why did you reject plausible alternative interpretations?
	• If the application of a rule to the relevant facts is not controversial, then do not spend a lot of time on it – do not create implausible alternative applications of the law for the sake of it.
	• However, a legal rule could be applied to the relevant facts in more than one genuinely plausible way – if this is the case, then you should reflect this in your analysis. If there is doubt, identify what this doubt relates to and provide your opinion on which of the plausible applications of law should be preferred.
Conclusion	• This stage is what students often miss out when answering problem questions, so ensure that you give it the attention that you gave to the other stages.
	• State what the answer to each legal issue should be, based on your application of the rules to the facts.
	• Offer an overall conclusion on the legal position of the person that you are advising, incorporating the outcomes of all of the legal issues raised by the problem question.
	• Sometimes, the conclusion you can give is relatively certain. Sometimes, your conclusion cannot be certain, but only likely or probable. Sometimes, your conclusion will have to be that the answers to the legal issues are uncertain and that there is more than one very plausible outcome.

Example:

Chapter 2 discussed how to plan your research and used the fact pattern involving Emily and Caden in order to illustrate these planning techniques. You will realise now that the examples used did many of the things from the IRAC framework. The practice of identifying the relevant legal issues, the relevant rule of law and what you will say in response to the legal issues is the heart of writing about law. You will be doing these things whatever the form of your assignment. The IRAC framework is simply a way of more formally and clearly structuring the way you do them when you are presented with a problem-style question. Thus, the plan for the response to Emily and Caden's fact pattern in Chapter 2 identified their issues, identified relevant rules, thought about how the rules would apply to the issues and also identified tentative conclusions on those issues. If you were answering this question for real, the next stage of the research process would be to go and do detailed reading, to work out if the law actually applies in the way you suspect it does, and to gather the detailed evidence that you would need to present when you write up your final argument on how the law should apply to Emily and Caden's issues. Here is a brief summary of how the work on Emily and Caden's fact pattern would fit into the IRAC framework.

Issues
- Does Emily owe a duty of care towards Caden?
- Does Emily meet the standard of care required to discharge her duty of care towards Caden, if she owes one?

Rule
- A duty of care exists where the parties are proximate, the damage is foreseeable and there are no public policy considerations to prevent the imposition of a duty of care.
- A *novus actus interveniens* can break the chain of causation between the plaintiff's actions and the defendant's injury, thus rendering the plaintiff not liable. To do so, the *novus actus interveniens* has to be outside the defendant's control and it must not have been something that the defendant should themselves have guarded against.
- A person bearing a duty of care must meet an objective standard of behaviour in order to discharge that duty and must behave in the way that a reasonable person would under the circumstances.
- If a defendant faced particularly pressurised circumstances or acted in a way that has high social utility, the assessment of whether they met the objective standard of behaviour required can be more lenient.

Application

- Emily and Caden are clearly proximate, but it is possible that Emily could not have foreseen all of Caden's actions or injuries as they ran. Nevertheless, she should have foreseen that running would create noise, which would alert the armed men. This in turn could lead to violence. She should then have foreseen that any violence might cause injury to Caden, who could then bleed uncontrollably due to his haemophilia. The throwing of the grenade was not outside of Emily's control – the man would clearly detonate the grenade if anyone in the area moved. There are no policy reasons to not impose a duty of care on Emily. Indeed, it would be beneficial for adults who are responsible for the care of children to be discouraged from 'playing the hero' in dangerous situations. Thus, a duty of care towards Caden should be imposed upon Emily.
- Emily did not act as a reasonable person would under the circumstances. In the circumstances that Emily faced, a reasonable person would have stayed put. He or she would have calculated that running would have provoked the armed men, who had made it clear that they would resort to violence if anyone moved. A reasonable person would have calculated that if violence ensued the risk of Caden sustaining life-threatening injuries due to his haemophilia would be high. Thus, Emily did not meet the objective standard of behaviour required to discharge the duty of care that she owed to Caden.

Conclusion

- It is likely that a court would conclude, based on the relevant applicable law, that Emily did owe Caden a duty of care and that she did not discharge that duty of care by attempting to run with him from the sports complex. Therefore, Emily should be liable for Caden's injuries.

Writing answers to problem questions is a skill that does not come overnight – you must practise, ideally with the support of a framework such as IRAC.

You may feel unsure when writing your first few problem question answers. You may find the process difficult. The bad news is that it will be difficult initially – you are being asked to write in a style with which you are probably unfamiliar. However, the good news is that answering problem questions gets easier with practice. You must, therefore, commit to practising this skill.

The more times you write an answer to a problem question using a framework such as IRAC, the better you will become at it. Take every opportunity to practise problem questions, including outside of your formal assessments.

- You should be able to access past exam papers for each of your law modules, whether through the website of your institution's library, or through the online learning spaces for the modules themselves.

- Core modules usually run small group tutorials, which often use problem questions as the basis for discussion. Treat the preparation for these seriously – the more you put into preparing for tutorials based on problem questions, the faster you will become good at answering problem questions.
- Finally, you may be able to get involved in free legal advice centres. These will allow you to deal with real-life legal problems and to provide reasoned and clearly articulated advice that answers the questions asked.

7.2 Dissertation proposals

7.2.1 What is a dissertation proposal?

A dissertation in law is an extended piece of legal writing. The length of dissertations will vary, but most undergraduate dissertations will be in the range of 8,000–12,000 words for a full-year dissertation, taught master's dissertations can be up to 20,000 words and research master's dissertations can be 50,000 words or more. If you write a dissertation at undergraduate or postgraduate level, you will not be given a question or assignment brief. You will need to come up with a topic yourself and you will need to construct a viable research question to investigate. You will then be expected to write a dissertation proposal in which you explain what your research question(s) is/are and how you plan to do the research required to answer any research question.[5]

The skills of forward planning, and of being able to explain a project's goals and how you will realise them, will be useful to you far beyond your dissertation. If you wish to undertake a PhD thesis, producing a research proposal will be necessary. Moreover, in the professional world, managers and supervisors will regularly make requests of you to update them on how you plan to achieve the work that you have been given. If you are self-employed, the ability to identify clear goals and a plan for how to realise them is essential.

---

[5] This section only discusses the process of writing a dissertation proposal. The whole process of dissertation writing, from conception to submission, is covered comprehensively in Michael Salter and Julie Mason, *Writing Law Dissertations: An Introduction and Guide to the Conduct of Legal Research* (Pearson 2007).

7.2.2 Choosing a topic

Before you begin writing a dissertation proposal, you must choose a dissertation topic. Every law student will be interested in different areas of law. Ask yourself what you have enjoyed studying the most so far, and whether there are any legal issues that you feel strongly about. Perhaps you have been following a story closely in the news, or a friend or family member has experienced some legal difficulty. Perhaps you yourself have been involved with a society or organisation whose work raises particular legal issues. Whatever your inspiration, you should try to think of a topic that you are interested in.

As an undergraduate or master's student, you do not necessarily have to come up with a project that will be ground-breaking. That is what the PhD thesis is for. However, you will be expected to show a command of the relevant legal field and a willingness to defend your opinions about the law in writing.

7.2.3 A research question for a dissertation proposal

So, how do you create a research question to investigate when you have no prompts whatsoever? Think of the process as like a funnel – you are starting from a wide topic of interest to you and trying to gradually narrow this down to a specific and feasible research question.

- Begin with a general area of law that interests you.
- Ask yourself whether there is anything about this topic that you find particularly interesting.
- Once you have identified something, ask yourself whether there are any specific issues within that more focussed area that you feel particularly passionate about or are particularly interested in.

Continue like this until you have reached a precise and clearly defined legal issue, problem, or unknown that you think could serve as a research question. Then, as discussed in Chapter 2, turn that issue into a question. Write it down somewhere and consider the essential parts or elements of that question. This process is represented in the graphic below.

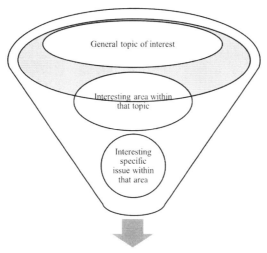

General topic of interest

Interesting area within that topic

Interesting specific issue within that area

Precise and clearly defined legal issue
– convert to a research question

7.2.4 Structuring a dissertation proposal

When you have identified a research question for your dissertation, you can then start to write your dissertation proposal. A good dissertation proposal will demonstrate that you:

- have a clear, focused and feasible legal research question to investigate and that you have thought in advance about what you might find in response to that research question;
- understand the field of law that your research question sits in;
- have thought about the practical steps (methodology) that will be required to rigorously investigate your research question; and
- have thought about the range of sources that you will need to refer to when you investigate your research question.

These correspond to the four essential elements of a research proposal.

(1) The abstract
- The abstract is ideally between 150 and 300 words and gives a summary of your research project.
- It should clearly identify your research question(s).
- It should identify the planned structure of your project and your potential lines of argument.
- It should give an indication of what you seek to achieve

with this project or what you broadly expect to find or show with your research.

(2) The legal context
- o The context section is where you demonstrate that you have done some background reading into your topic and that you have a good initial grasp of the law that is relevant to your research question(s).
- o It needs to provide an overview of the legal field within which your project sits – identify important legislation and case law that is relevant to your research question(s), give an indication of the key academic commentary that is relevant to your research question, identify any recent developments in policy or proposed legal reforms that are relevant to your research question(s).
- o Ideally, it should also identify any knowledge gaps in the relevant legal field – are there any relevant legal or policy problems that academic commentary has not yet addressed and will your dissertation address or touch upon any of these issues? It is always a good idea to show that you understand where the gaps in knowledge exist and what impact this might have upon how you go about answering your chosen research question.

(3) The methodology
- o The methodology section is where you outline the type of legal analysis that you will perform in the dissertation and any important practical steps that you will take in doing this analysis. Types of methodology include doctrinal, socio-legal, historical and comparative – you should provide an indication of which type of methodology (or methodologies) you will be following.
- o It should indicate the key sources and databases that you plan to use and indicate whether there are any specialised processes that you need to undertake (for example, gaining ethical approval for your project if it raises research ethics issues).
- o It should also ideally provide an indication of any key foreseeable challenges that you might encounter during your research and how you plan to overcome these (for example, any anticipated difficulties in obtaining essential source material).

(4) The bibliography
- o The bibliography section is one that you will be familiar with already. Here you list the sources that you have referred to in your legal context section and any other

source material that you think will be important to your research.

- o Putting effort into the bibliography of your dissertation proposal will save you time later on. It will provide a starting list of sources that you can go and read when you conduct your detailed research. It will also be a starting template for the bibliography that you will eventually need to include at the end of your dissertation.

Your dissertation proposal should be treated as a living document and the base from which you conduct your dissertation research. Writing a dissertation is a long exercise and you may find that after a few months of doing detailed research on a topic you have strayed from your planned focus. Your proposal will help you to re-orient yourself towards the research that is relevant to answering your research question(s). As identified above, some parts of your proposal will be useful templates for aspects of the dissertation itself when you come to write it, in particular the methodology and bibliography sections. Writing the legal context section of your proposal will help to give you a running start on the type of detailed research that you will need to conduct during your dissertation project, and can provide an early indication of any elements of your research question that are going to be particularly challenging to investigate. Treat the writing of your dissertation proposal not just as an exercise that is forced upon you, but as an opportunity to develop essential professional skills and provide yourself with an anchor and platform from which to write the best dissertation possible.

7.2.5 Dissertation proposal layout

Your institution may have a prescribed dissertation proposal layout. In the absence of institutional guidance, ensure that your dissertation proposal is presented in a way that is easy to read, covers the essential elements of a research proposal and is a useful guide for both you and your supervisor.

Ensure that you reflect the elements of good legal writing outlined in this book – keep your sentences short, cover one topic per paragraph, use headings to guide the reader through your proposal and proofread your proposal before submission.

Set out below is a template dissertation proposal.

Dissertation research proposal

[*Name and Student Number*]

Proposed dissertation title:
[*While your dissertation title may evolve during the course of your research, try to pick an initial proposed title that is an accurate reflection of what you want to research. This may be used as the basis for allocating you a supervisor*]

Research abstract:
[*Outline **what** you want to research and what it is that you want to find out about that topic (rather than just discussing the topic generally) – what question or questions do you intend to answer or prove through your research?*]

Legal context:
[*Give more details about what you propose to research. Provide context for, and give some background to, your proposed research topic. **Where** does your research fit within this? What is the aim of your research? Are there any specific legal issues or themes that you anticipate being relevant to your research?*]

Methodology:
[***How** do you plan to conduct your research? Will your research be mainly doctrinal in nature? Will there be a comparative, socio-legal and/or interdisciplinary element? Will there be any data analysis required?*]

Ethical issues:
[*Based on your methodology, indicate if you anticipate there being any ethical issues raised by your research – for example, do you plan on conducting interviews?*]

Initial resources/bibliography:
[*Set out a list of some key resources that you will be consulting – this does not need to be extensive, but should cover the main resources that you think may be relevant.*]

7.3 Letters

You may query the ongoing relevance of letters in your university and professional life. While email has certainly superseded letters as the most common form of written communication, there is still a place for letters. You might write a cover letter to a potential employer, as part of (real or fictional) court submissions, to communicate to solicitors on the other side of a transaction, or to set out legal advice for a client.

When you are writing a letter in a professional context, your employer may have a letter template that will include your employer's logo and any required regulatory information. If such a template exists, make sure that you use it for any business-related letters that you are writing. While the guidance below is intended to apply to all letters, anything contradictory in your employer's template or house style should override this guidance.

7.3.1 Structuring a letter

(1) **Address details, date and reference:** The top of a letter will include basic information.
- **First:** the address details of the sender should be aligned to the right-hand side of the page. Do not include your name. If you are sending a letter in a professional context, this address will be your employer's name and address.
- **Second:** leave a blank line after the sender's address and include your telephone number and email address (if you are signing the letter) or the telephone number and email address of whoever is signing the letter (if you are writing the letter on someone else's behalf).
- **Third:** the recipient's full name and address should be aligned to the left-hand side of the page.
- **Fourth:** leave a blank line and add in any reference number (this is only relevant if you are writing a letter at work and your employer catalogues documents by client and matter numbers).
- **Fifth:** leave a blank line and add the date on which the letter is being signed.

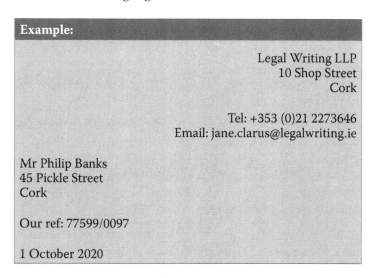

Example:

Legal Writing LLP
10 Shop Street
Cork

Tel: +353 (0)21 2273646
Email: jane.clarus@legalwriting.ie

Mr Philip Banks
45 Pickle Street
Cork

Our ref: 77599/0097

1 October 2020

(2) **Greeting:** Include an appropriate greeting in a letter and keep it formal. This greeting will start with 'Dear', never 'Hi' or 'Hey'.

- If you know the recipient's name, but have not contacted him or her before, address him or her by title and surname (for example: 'Dear Mr Banks').
- If you have a working relationship with the recipient, you might consider referring to him or her by first name (for example: 'Dear Philip').
- If you do not know the recipient's name (which might be the case if your letter is addressed to the person holding a particular position, such as Director of Human Resources), then address the letter to 'Dear Sir' or 'Dear Madam' (if you know the recipient's gender) or 'Dear Sir or Madam' (if you do not).

(3) **Subject line:** After your greeting, leave a blank line and include the subject of your letter in bold.

Subject lines should be short but informative. They should allow the reader to quickly identify what the letter relates to without having to read the whole letter. If the envelope that you are using has a clear plastic window for the address, make sure that the subject line of the letter is *not* visible through this window.

(4) **Body of the letter:** Your letter should start with an introductory sentence in which you explain what the letter is about. This does not need to be an extensive discussion, but rather a helpful reminder to the recipient.

The remainder of your letter should be divided into paragraphs – a letter that is one long paragraph will be difficult for the recipient to understand. Try to deal with one point per paragraph and consider including headings and sub-headings to help reader comprehension. See Section 5.4.3 above for a discussion about using headings.

Where you are writing a cover letter (or similar), check whether you are told what information needs to be included in the letter (and make sure you include it) and whether there is a maximum page or word count imposed. Cover letters are often limited to one page.

As with all good legal writing, try to keep the sentences in your letters short and the language as clear and simple as is needed in the context. Remember, if you are sending a letter to a third party or a client, he or she may not have any legal training. That recipient is, therefore, unlikely to understand complex legal terminology, archaic legal phrases or uncommon Latin expressions. Think about what the recipient wants from your letter. If the recipient does not need a lot of background or a lot of technical detail, then consider omitting this. If they need an outline of different options, make sure these are clearly laid out.

Letters sent to clients and third parties in the context of legal negotiations are subject to additional regulatory requirements and may contain phrases and disclaimers that impact the legal effect of the letter. These aspects of letters are beyond the scope of this book.

(5) **A complementary close and signature:** The close of your letter should complement the greeting in terms of style. The two options for closing a letter are 'Yours sincerely' or 'Yours faithfully'. The correct close will depend on whether your greeting included the recipient's name or not.

Greeting	Complementary close
Dear Sir/Dear Madam/Dear Sir or Madam	Yours faithfully
Dear [*name*]	Yours sincerely

After the close of your letter, leave four or five blank lines (this is where the letter will be signed) and add the sender's full name in bold. In the next line, add the sender's status. This will be the sender's job title (if the letter is being written in a professional context) or the sender's qualifications (if the sender is a student).

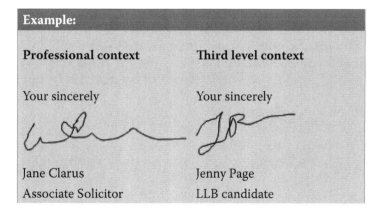

Example:

Professional context

Your sincerely

Jane Clarus
Associate Solicitor

Third level context

Your sincerely

Jenny Page
LLB candidate

(6) **Copied recipients:** There may be situations where you need to send a copy of a letter to another recipient for their information (for example, if you are sending a letter to the court and want

to send a copy of this letter to the other side). If you intend to send copies of the letter to other people, you should specify this at the end of the letter by writing 'Copy to' or 'Cc' and the names of those people. Do remember to then actually send them a copy of the letter.

(7) **Enclosures:** If you are including any documents in the envelope with your letter, make sure that you list these documents in the body of your letter and include the abbreviation 'Encl' at the end of your letter.

7.3.2 Headings, lists and optics

Headings will help you to structure your letter in a way that is clear and easy to understand. Where a letter is more than five paragraphs long consider including headings to divide up the various sections. These headings should accurately reflect the substance of the paragraphs that follow. In this way, headings can help to guide the recipient through the substance of the letter and can highlight those sections of the letter that require action by the recipient (for example: 'Next Steps' or 'Information to be Provided').

If you include headings in a letter, make sure there are no 'orphan' headings, where the heading is left dangling at the bottom of a page with the related paragraphs pushed to the next page. If you have an orphan heading, move it to the next page. On Microsoft Word, you can also tick the 'Keep with next' option in the Paragraph settings tab. This will force orphan headings onto the same page as the next related paragraph.

Lists in letters can be useful when setting out information that the recipient needs to understand clearly – number these lists, rather than using bullet points. Use numbered lists when you are listing documents enclosed in the letter, when you are setting out steps that need to be taken or when you are setting out different options.

Finally, consider the optics of your letter.

- Make sure the font is one that is easy to read (Times New Roman or Arial) and is the same throughout the document.
- Use a consistent font size (font-size 11 or 12 depending on the font used).
- Check that all paragraphs are evenly spaced, that any lists are sequential and that headings are consistent in appearance.

- Add page numbers if your letter is more than one page long.
- Justify the alignment of your text (other than the address details).

7.3.3 Tone

The tone of your letter will be determined by the purpose of the letter. A letter of advice to a client who is bereaved should be sympathetic and calm, a letter to the court should be succinct and matter of fact. Whatever tone you adopt, you must always remain professional and respectful. A letter is not the medium for displaying anger or annoyance. You should never, therefore, be rude, aggressive or sarcastic in a letter (or, indeed, in any means of communication). That letter can be photocopied, scanned or stored away only to be produced at a later date – think carefully about what you include in it.

If a letter is an important one (for example, a cover letter to a potential employer) ask someone else to read the letter before you send it. This will help you to adopt an appropriate tone and level of professionalism.

7.3.4 Letter template

Set out below is a template letter. Information to be amended is included in square brackets.

[*Address of sender*]

Tel: [*full telephone number of sender*]
Email: [*email address of sender*]

[*Name of recipient*]
[*Address of recipient*]

Our ref: [*if relevant*]

[*Date*]

Dear [*name or appropriate noun*]

[*Subject of letter*]

Thank you for your letter dated [*insert date*][*if you are replying in a chain of correspondence*]

I write to you with respect to [*background/reason for writing*].

[*Set out the body of your letter in paragraphs. Keep your sentences short and clear. Use headings and numbered lists to aid comprehension*].

[*If you want the recipient to do anything, make this clear. If you enclose any documents, make sure that you list them*].

[Yours sincerely]/[Yours faithfully]

[*Sender's name*]
[*Sender's status*]

Copy to: [*name*][*if relevant*]

Encl [*if relevant*]

7.4 Emails

In our studies, and in our professional and personal lives email is now one of our main methods of communication. It can be easy to view emails as a quick way of conveying a message without the need for appropriate formality or attention. All too often, people do not distinguish between personal and professional emails – this can lead to emails that are inappropriately familiar, unprofessional or even impolite.

If you are sending an email to someone other than your friends or family, you should observe rules of professional email etiquette.

These are relevant if you are emailing your lecturer, a potential employer, a colleague or a client. Treat emails as a piece of formal writing and apply the rules discussed in this book to your emails in the same way that you would for any other piece of legal writing.

Employers are less likely to have a template form of email than they are to have a template form of letter. If such a template exists, you should use it in conjunction with your employer's house style.

7.4.1 Some basic email tips

(1) **Is the email necessary and appropriate?** Before you send an email, consider whether an email is the best method of communication in the context.

An email is only necessary if its purpose cannot be addressed in some other way. Do not, for example, email your lecturer asking about the date of the exam, when this information is easily found in the course handbook.

You should also avoid sending anything inappropriate or unprofessional by email (particularly using an institutional email address). Remember, an email is a written record that can be backed up, saved, forwarded and printed. Never send anything by email that you would not be comfortable having read back to you at a later date.

(2) **Always check the recipients' email addresses and that they are in the right address field:** This seems obvious, but you do not want your email sent to the incorrect recipients. As a result, always double check recipients' email addresses. This is particularly important if you regularly email different people with the same first name. If you do not pay attention your email system may suggest the wrong person when you start typing his or her name into the address field.

Consider in which address field your recipients should be included.
- 'To': The person or people to whom the email is primarily intended should be included in the 'To' field and the text of the email addressed to him/her/them.
- 'Cc' (carbon copy): Other people who are not expected to reply to the email, but who you think should receive a copy of it (for example, your supervisor at work) are included in the 'Cc' field. Their email addresses will be visible to other recipients of the email.
- 'Bcc' (blind carbon copy): If you include someone in

the 'Bcc' field, no one else on the email will know that he or she has been copied. This may be useful if you are emailing a large group of people and do not feel it is appropriate to display everyone's email address. However, please be aware that if someone replies 'All' to your email, those people who have been Bcc'd will *not* be included in the reply.

(3) **Check all attachments before sending:** It can be easy to attach the wrong document to an email, particularly if you have documents that have been saved on your computer with unhelpful names.

The first thing you should do to avoid this issue is to make sure that when you save documents, you give them names that are easy to understand and distinguish. Do not just rely on the file name that your computer suggests. If you have multiple versions of the same document, make sure their file name includes the date (and even the time, if you save multiple versions in a day) so that you can quickly identify the most recent one. Saving documents with helpful names also makes it easier for the recipients of your email to work out what each document is.

Open every document attached to your email before you click send. This is to make sure that you have attached all of the correct documents. Whenever you are attaching documents to an email, it is helpful to list these documents in the email – as you open each attachment, make sure the relevant document is correct and that it is listed in your email.

Whenever you send an attachment to someone, include a brief indication of what is attached in the email – never send a blank email containing only an attachment.

Finally, be conscious of the size of your attachments. Email systems usually have maximum limits on attachments above which the email will not be delivered. If you are sending multiple documents, which together are likely to exceed any maximum file size limit, send these over the course of several emails (with reference in the subject field to the number of emails that will be sent and the number of each email in that series (for example: 'Signed Documents | Project Car (email 1 of 3)').

(4) **Be professional and polite:** Emails sent to someone other than a friend or family member should always be professional and

polite. Do not abandon the formalities of professional writing just because you are communicating by email.

As a result, your emails should reflect the following.

- **Structure your email like a letter:** Every email should have an initial greeting, a substantive body and a final sign off. See Section 7.4.3 below for more details on email structure.

- **Write your email like a letter:** Increasingly, students seem to avoid using punctuation, capital letters and correct grammar in emails. It is not uncommon now to receive an email that contains no capital letters, full stops or commas. This looks extremely sloppy and suggests to the email recipient that you could not be bothered to write correctly. Such emails can also be hard to understand. Please take the time to ensure that you write in full sentences, that you add capital letters where appropriate and that you include punctuation.

- **Do not use capital letters for emphasis:** Writing something all in capital letters will appear rude and demanding. If you want to emphasise a particular word, italicise it.

- **Always avoid text speak, slang or emojis/emoticons:** While you may occasionally get an email from your supervisor at work that simply says 'pls deal, thx', you should avoid using colloquial language in an email. This includes any kind of text speak, slang and emojis or emoticons – no professional email ever ended with a smiley face.

- **Use abbreviated language carefully:** As a general rule, abbreviations (such as HTH (hope that helps), BTW (by the way), EoD (end of day), FYI (for your information)) should be avoided, particularly when you are emailing your lecturer, supervisor or a client. However, you may find that once you enter a professional context, abbreviations are used quite often in internal emails. When in doubt, write the full phrase.

- **Do not demand a reply (unless appropriate in the context):** Before you demand a reply or set a deadline in an email, think about whether the recipient is already aware of the urgency or whether there is, in fact, no urgency. If the recipient is aware of the urgency, telling him or her about it risks causing annoyance. If there is no urgency, demanding a reply will appear rude. As a result, unless something is urgent and the recipient is not aware of this urgency, avoid ending your email with anything that demands a prompt reply (for example: 'Please reply at your earliest convenience' or similar).

(5) **If the email contains a request or instruction, be clear at whom this is directed:** If your email asks someone to do something or to provide something, that person should generally be listed in the 'To' address field and his or her name included in the email greeting.

There may be situations where an email is addressed to multiple people and you have individual requests or instructions to give different people. Here, make sure that you indicate who needs to do what – the best way to do this is to name the relevant person, include his or her name in bold and then clearly set out the request or instructions for that person.

Example:

From: jane.clarus@legalwriting.ie
Sent: 29 September 2020 9:01
To: jon.lock@legalwriting.ie; matt.balm@legalwriting.ie
Subject: Conference | 28 September 2020 | Document

Dear All

Please find attached the document discussed at yesterday's conference. We will be discussing this in detail in my office at 2pm today.

Jon, please could you print this out and bring it to my office ahead of today's meeting.

Matt, if you could please check the outstanding point we discussed yesterday, that would be great.

Kind regards

Jane

---

(6) **Always proofread an email, even a short one:** Like other pieces of legal writing, you should proofread every email before clicking 'send'. This applies even to short emails. You want to avoid including a typo or other mistake in an email. You also want to avoid writing something in anger that you later regret. Take the time to read and reflect on what the email is saying. For longer emails or any important emails, it is a good idea to print the email out and proofread it in hard copy.

Finally, if your email system has a built-in delay function, consider turning this on. This can provide a short delay on sending your emails after you click 'send', allowing you to cancel the sending. This can be helpful if, despite your proofreading, you notice a mistake after you have clicked 'send'.

(7) **Use headings, lists and numbered points:** Headings, lists and numbered points can be very useful in making your emails easy to read and understand.

For longer emails, where there are a number of issues discussed, consider breaking these up with useful headings – this will allow each recipient to quickly identify what is being covered in the email and what is relevant to him or her.

Using short paragraphs and breaking long sentences into lists will allow the recipient to extract the relevant information quickly without having to re-read your email. Do make sure that when you include a list, that each point is numbered (rather than bullet pointed). This way, if the recipient wants to refer to a specific point in their reply email or over the phone, they can just refer to the number, rather than awkwardly directing you down a list of bullet points.

Example:

From: jane.clarus@legalwriting.ie
Sent: 29 September 2020 16:20
To: jon.lock@legalwriting.ie; matt.balm@legalwriting.ie
Subject: Conference | 28 September 2020 | Document

Dear All

Thank you for your time this afternoon.

Follow up items with client
As discussed at the 2pm meeting, I will raise the following points with our client:
1. the relevance of the new legislation;
2. the date scheduled for the next conference; and
3. the spelling mistake on page 4 of the document.

Next meeting
I will set up a meeting with the partner for 3pm tomorrow.

Kind regards
Jane

(8)   **Use consistent font, colour and paragraph spacing throughout:** Like other pieces of legal writing, the optics of an email are important.

Avoid using unusual or hard to read fonts in your emails. A standard default font used in emails is Arial, font size 10 in black throughout the text of the email.

If you copy and paste text from another source, make sure that it is in the same colour and font as the rest of your email. Before pressing 'send' on an email, therefore, highlight the text of your email and check that everything is the same size, font and colour. Also check to make sure that paragraphs are consistently spaced, and that any numbered lists are sequential.

7.4.2 Security issues with emails

(1)   **Read and familiarise yourself with any email policies published by your institution or employer:** Your institution or employer is likely to have a printed policy on email good practice and security. Read a copy of this policy and make sure that you comply with it.

(2)   **Do not assume an email is private – it can always be forwarded to others:** Be careful about including sensitive or unprofessional information in an email – there is nothing to stop the recipient printing or forwarding that email to someone else (even if they are not supposed to).

(3)   **If you have an institutional email address (that is, one provided by your university, other third-level institution or employer), try to use that:** Students frequently use their personal email addresses when emailing lecturers. This may be a breach of your third-level institution's email policies. If you have an institutional email address, you should always use that for emails related to your studies. Students sometimes include their personal email address on their CV and cover letters. While there is nothing wrong with doing this, be cautious about doing so if your personal email address looks unprofessional. An email address that contains just your first and last names (or some variation of this) is fine, one that contains inappropriate, offensive or childish words is probably not.

Once you enter a professional environment, use your institutional work email address for business emails. Again, it is likely to be a breach of your employer's email policy for you to be conducting work-related activity through your personal email address.

7.4.3 Structuring an email

A good email is one that is well laid out and whose contents are easy to understand.

(1) **Subject line:** Always include a subject line in your emails – it should never be left blank. Subject lines should be short but informative and should allow the reader to quickly identify what the email relates to. If you are working on a confidential matter at work that uses a project name, include that in the subject line – do not identify the project's parties in the subject line.

When you reply to an email, retain the subject line if the reply relates to the original email. If, however, you want to send the same recipients an email on an unrelated topic, remember to change the subject line (and ideally start a new email chain). It is very confusing if the subject line bears no relationship to the subject of the email.

(2) **Greeting:** Start your email with a polite greeting. You would never start a letter without a greeting and the same rule applies to an email. There is a growing trend of people not including a greeting in emails and simply launching into the content of the email. Avoid doing this – no matter how pressed for time you are, it is good practice to include a greeting.

The type of greeting used will depend on your relationship with the recipient and previous interaction by email.
- The first time you email someone in a professional or academic context, start your email with 'Dear' and then the person's first or surname. 'Hi [*name*]' is generally not appropriate in an initial email unless you have a working relationship with someone.
- Only default to 'Hi [*name*]' in subsequent emails if the recipient replies to your email using 'Hi'.
- 'Heya [*name*]', 'Hiya [*name*]' or 'Hey [*name*]' will never be appropriate in this context. Please do not email your lecturers, colleagues or clients using these greetings.
- Some people choose to avoid a greeting and simply include the person's first name (for example, rather than writing: 'Dear Professor Smith', just writing 'Professor

Smith'). There is nothing wrong with this, although it can appear a little abrupt.

- If you are emailing a group of people, include all of their names if you are emailing up to three people (for example: 'Dear Penelope, Jack and Mohammed'). If you are emailing a larger number of people, use an appropriate collective noun or pronoun (for example: 'Dear All', 'Dear Colleagues', 'Dear Accounts Team').

> **Practical Tip:**
>
> When in doubt as to what greeting to use in an email, it is always safest to err on the side of formality. No one will mind receiving an email with a formal greeting. However, you may offend someone with an overly casual one.

As part of the greeting, make sure that you spell the recipient's name correctly. Particularly if someone has an unusual name, or his or her name has an unusual spelling, carefully check that each letter is correct. You have the recipient's name in front of you – there is absolutely no excuse for misspelling it.

(3) **Body of the email:** Avoid including superfluous information in an email. The body of your email should get your message across clearly and quickly.

Start with a short introduction to explain why you are sending the email. If you have not had contact with the person before, it is usually helpful to introduce yourself (for example, 'I am a student in your 2nd year LLB legal writing class', 'I am a trainee solicitor in Daisy Smith's restructuring team at Legal Writing LLP'). This avoids the recipient having to work out who you are.

The remainder of your email should be broken down into short paragraphs. These paragraphs can be shorter than those included in a letter (and may, in practice, be one or two sentences long). As with all legal writing, each paragraph should deal with one main idea. Get to the main point of your email in the first paragraph after your introduction (for example: 'I have set out below the steps that will need to be taken ahead of the postgraduate open day') and avoid giving unnecessary background information. People have little patience for long rambling emails. If your email contains substantive advice that you need the recipient to read carefully, it may be most effective to present this advice in the form of a standalone letter or memorandum that is saved as a

PDF and attached to your email (with the body of your email simply giving an indication of what is attached).

Where your email is asking a series of questions, setting out steps, or highlighting a number of issues, include these as a numbered list.

(4) **Sign off and signature block:** Like the greeting in an email, always sign off your emails.

The method of sign off will depend on your relationship with the recipient and should match the level of formality in your greeting (for example, if you start an email with 'Dear Professor Smith', you should not be ending it with 'Ta muchly').

- The safest way to end an email is with 'Yours sincerely' (if it is a very formal email) or, more commonly, some variation of 'Kind regards' (if it is a standard business email).
- 'Yours faithfully' is usually too formal for an email unless you do not know the name of the recipients and you have addressed the email 'Dear Sir or Madam'.
- If you have a working relationship with the recipient (that is, if you use 'Hi' in your greeting) and your email includes a request, you can consider using 'Many thanks'.
- Avoid writing 'Thanks in advance' or similar as this suggests that you expect the recipient to do something for you.
- Do not use an overly casual sign off, such as 'Cheers', 'Thx' or the dreaded 'xx'.

As your full name will show up in the 'From' field of an email, it usually enough to sign off your email with your first name. If you think the recipient may not know who you are, you can include your full name (and, if you are a student, include your student number).

If your institution has a standard signature block (which includes your name, job title and contact details) include this on all emails sent externally.

(5) **Attachments:** Open all attachments before you click 'send' and make sure that every document that you intend to attach is attached. See Section 7.4.1 above for more discussion on attachments.

7.4.4 Replying to an email

(1) **When to reply:** Everyone receives a lot of emails. If an email is sent to you for your information only and does not invite a response, you do not need to reply.

Where it is clear that you are expected to reply to an email, do so relatively promptly. Emails should ideally be replied to on the day that they are received, and always within 24 hours of receipt (unless it is clear from the email that a response is not expected for some time). If you do not reply to emails promptly you increase the risk that an individual email will get pushed down in your inbox and you will forget about it.

(2) **Holding responses:** Not replying promptly to an email could lead the sender to question whether you have received the email. If you receive an email that invites a response, but you are unable to respond within 24 hours, it is good practice to send a 'holding response'. A holding response is a reply email in which you confirm that you have received the email and that you will respond. You can also explain why you will not be responding immediately (for example: 'Many thanks for sending us the draft transaction documents. We will review these and, after confirming the outstanding information with our client, we will send you any comments that we and our client have.').

(3) **How to reply:** When you reply to an email, provide responses to the questions asked and confirm whether the steps outlined have been taken. As with original emails, ensure that your paragraphs are short and helpful, that your text is all in the same font and that you include an appropriate greeting and sign off.

When you reply to an email, do not delete the email chain that contains the original email (and any subsequent correspondence). This is important for context and to avoid confusing the recipient. If, however, you are adding additional recipients to your reply email, read through the email chain to make sure there is nothing that the new recipients should not be sent.

If there is something in the original email that angers you, avoid snapping in your reply. Remain professional and calm in your reply – emails are not a place to trade insults.

(4) **Beware the 'reply all':** Clicking the 'reply all' button when you reply means that the sender, everyone in the original 'To' field

and everyone in the 'Cc' field will receive your reply. While this might be appropriate where your answer is of relevance to everyone on the email, be careful before clicking 'reply all'.

Consider who needs to receive your reply – it may just be the sender. However, where the 'Cc' field of the email includes the sender's colleagues or supervisor, it is usually a good idea to copy them in on your reply to avoid the recipient having to forward your reply email to them.

7.4.5 Email template

Set out below is a template email. Information to be amended is included in square brackets.

From:	[*your email address*]
Sent:	[*email date*]
To:	[*recipients that the email is addressed to – check carefully*]
Cc:	[*recipients that the email is being sent to for their information – check carefully*]
Bcc:	[*recipients whose email addresses will not be visible to anyone else – check carefully*]
Subject:	[*the email's subject should be short, helpful and relevant to the email's contents*]

Dear/Hi [*name*]/All/[*appropriate noun*]

[*Introduction – explain who you are and/or why you are sending this email*].

[*Include appropriate headings for longer emails*]
1. [*Add in numbered lists where you are referring to a number of questions, steps, tasks or documents.*]

Kind regards/Yours sincerely/Many thanks

[*your first name*]
[*add in your student number, if relevant*]

[*ensure that you include your institutional signature block if you have one*]

7.5 Presentations

Presentations are not typically covered in books about legal research and writing. However, a presentation involves more than just making oral arguments. A presentation is just as rigorous and serious a test of your research and communication skills as an essay or an exam.[6]

There is a structured method to doing an oral presentation using visual aids such as slides. This is because a presentation, in which you communicate your research findings and arguments orally, is quite a different entity to the written essay. If you do not adopt a structured approach to a presentation task, then what comes out of your mouth on the day of the presentation will likely be far less coherent and impactful than it could be. As such, it will not be a good reflection of what you think and what you know.

There are three stages of good presentation methodology:
- the research stage, in which you gather the information you will need;
- the preparation stage, in which you turn your research notes into a series of easy to follow points and prepare visual aids to accompany these points; and
- the delivery stage, in which you deliver your arguments to an audience using a combination of oral and visual communication.

This section will focus on the research and written elements of a presentation – two aspects that are so often overlooked or considered less important than the oral portion of a presentation.

7.5.1 The research stage – conducting your research

Before you dive into your research, there are some preliminary questions to consider, the answers to which will help your presentation to assume the right character.

- What does the title or the topic that you have been given suggest about the aim of the presentation? Are you supposed to be giving a broad overview of a topic or are you drilling down into a specific part of that topic? You have much less space and time available in a presentation, so it is important that you know exactly what you should be using your time to achieve.
- Who will the audience be? Can you assume that your audience has a certain level of legal knowledge or are

---

[6] On the importance of law students developing good oral advocacy skills generally, see: Samuel H Pillsbury, 'Valuing the Spoken Word: Public Speaking for Lawyers' (2006) 34 Capital University Law Review 517; Jane Korn, 'Teaching Talking: Oral Communication Skills in a Law Course' (2004) 54 Journal of Legal Education 588.

you meant to assume that your audience knows nothing about the legal topic on which you are presenting? Again, this is important to know, so that you do not tell your audience things that they already know.

- How interesting is the topic? If you are giving the same presentation as everyone else, how can you give yours a different edge while still addressing the question properly? If the audience is bored and completely disengages from your presentation, you will find it much harder to get your arguments across clearly and purposefully. Thus, it is important that you ensure from the outset that your presentation is likely to grab and hold the audience's interest.

Once you have given some thought to these initial points, and prepared accordingly, you can begin researching. The research skills required for a presentation are no different to those required for a written assignment. The same processes of beginning, finding and reading information should be used.

(1) **Effective note taking:** Effective note taking is important when you conduct research for a presentation. You do not want your presentation to consist of large chunks of text copied from your notes – this will be boring for the audience and will not deliver your arguments effectively. Try to avoid this possibility by putting extra effort into taking effective notes, rather than simply copying and summarising what the sources say. Write down the questions you find yourself asking when reading and write down what you think and feel in response to your reading. It will also make it easier to create and successfully convey a specific and interesting line of argument. If you do summarise information within a source, with a view to including it in your presentation, write these summaries in your own words – your oral communication of this information will then at least sound natural, rather than regurgitated from the pages of a book.

(2) **Referencing:** Delivering a presentation does not negate the need to acknowledge your sources of information or ideas. You should, therefore, provide appropriate reference information for any quotes or similar material (such as charts or diagrams) included in slides or in a handout. As a result, you need to record where your information and ideas came from. Do not be tempted to think that the presentation is a less rigorous test of your research ability than an essay and that you are

therefore excused from the obligation to give credit to sources where necessary in a presentation – it is not, and you are not.

(3) **Flexibility of available source:** One aspect of conducting research for a presentation is slightly different. You have more flexibility in how you present information in a presentation – you can use graphics, videos, graphs or other more interactive visual aids. As a result, you should be more alert to the possibility that information contained in pictures and graphs might be useful to you. This is information that you might overlook when researching an essay, so when you are researching a presentation remind yourself that a wider range of information is worth thinking about and recording. Remember that your audience can take in visual information on your slides at the same time as listening to you.

7.5.2 The preparation stage – preparing your visual aids

The preparation stage is where the presentation methodology diverges from the essay or problem question methodology. When you write an essay, you plan your arguments and sources, do the required detailed research and then proceed directly to writing your essay – once your essay is written, you proofread it and at this point it is essentially finished. When you conduct a presentation, you still plan your arguments and sources, and do the required detailed research, but you must not then assume that you can simply proceed to deliver the presentation on the day. You must prepare for this delivery. In addition to preparing to deliver your oral arguments, you may also prepare visual aids for your audience that support the delivery of your arguments.

(1) **Basic considerations when using visual aids:** Most presenters choose the traditional PowerPoint presentation as their visual aid, however this is not the only form of visual aid that is acceptable – other presentation software is commonly used, as well as handouts, projections or props. Whatever visual aids you choose to employ, remember that whenever you put something in front of an audience, you are inviting them to look at it. This means that you should ensure that your visual aids complement the information you are communicating orally and do not distract from it. Your visual aids should also follow the rules of good legal writing discussed in this book – make sure you use short sentences, avoid unnecessary Latin words or complicated phrases.

(2) **Consider what you want the audience to read:** There are several things to consider when preparing your visual aids,

but whatever you do, try to avoid putting large amounts of text in front of your audience unless it is really essential (for example, the wording of a statutory provision, or a key quote from a judgment, which you are directly analysing). Your audience will not pay attention to what you are saying if they are trying to read lines of text. Your oral argument should be the complete presentation and the visual aids should be used to enhance this oral argument. You should, therefore, use visual aids to give the audience extra bits of information to supplement your oral argument and to save you having to read out certain key passages of text in full. However, you do not want to get to the point where there is more information in your slides than there is in your oral argument.

With the above in mind, there are four reasons why you would use visual aids, such as PowerPoint slides, in presentations. Ensure that your visual aids are achieving one or more of these, otherwise they may distract from your argument.

(a) **Visual aids can be used to assist understanding, to make complex information that you are talking about more comprehensible to your audience.** For example, if you are talking about complex statistics, then your audience's understanding would be enhanced if you provided them with a helpful graph that puts the statistics in a more comprehensible format.

(b) **Visual aids can provide information that you want your audience to have, but which you do not want to include in your oral delivery.** For example, you might want the audience to know that the arguments that you are currently speaking about are informed by particular pieces of literature – rather than waste time mentioning these one by one, you could put them on a slide. This lets the audience know that you are crediting your work properly, but does not interrupt the flow of your argument. While audience members do not want to read large sections of text, they are capable of reading essential text as they listen to your argument.

(c) **Visual aids can engage the audience's interest.** This can be particularly important if your presentation is on more technical topics. Visual cues, such as a well-chosen picture or a relevant quote, can be used to attract and hold the audience's attention.

(d) **Finally, visual aids can be used to add clarity to your presentation.** Diagrams and bullet point lists can be very helpful in summarising detailed lines of argument or visualising constituent elements of a wider concept. Pointing at a diagram as you explain a complicated concept allows the audience to see how different parts of that concept relate to each other. It also means that the audience are more likely to remember your explanation as you progress through it. Another important visual aid you could use in this respect is a bullet point list outlining the structure of your presentation at the start, which you can refer back to as you move through the presentation.

Presenters can fall into a number of common traps when preparing visual aids for a presentation, which largely happens as a result of not taking the time to think about how visual aids can most effectively be used.

- Presenters may rush the preparation of visual aids and assume that as long as they are there, they will be useful. This is not true. Your audience will judge you on the quality of your visual aids, as well as on the quality of your oral argument. As with any piece of legal writing, dedicate time to preparing clear, helpful and well-planned visual aids for your presentations.
- Presenters may try to make their visual aids too technologically complex. This is not helpful. A simple PowerPoint presentation can enhance your oral communication if it is designed to support rather than distract from your argument. What does not impress the audience is seeing a presenter struggling with visual aids that they cannot get to work or have forgotten how to operate.
- Presenters may overload slides with complex information. Presenters may believe that, if they cannot get everything they know into their oral argument, they can shove it into their slides. In practice:
    - first: A good legal presentation demonstrates that you can analyse and evaluate the law – putting slides full of information in front of your audience will not help you to show this;
    - second: Whenever you put something in front of an audience, you invite them to look at it – if the audience has spent the whole of your presentation reading and deciphering what is on your slides, and not listening to what you are saying, you will have failed to fulfil the purpose of the

presentation, which is to orally communicate a clear and memorable argument.

- Presenters may use unusual fonts or a lot of different colours on slides, because they think that this is the best way to attract and hold the audience's attention. Consider, however, what the audience can actually see. For example, the audience might not be able to read text that is in a small and curly font, or be able to see yellow, light green or light blue text on a white background. Be aware of your audience's physical limitations and put visual aids in front of them that they are able to comfortably process.

After you have prepared your visual aids, you must devote your attention to one last aspect of the preparation stage – practising your presentation. You absolutely do not want the first time you deliver your presentation to be during the actual presentation itself. Practising your presentation is also an opportunity to test your visual aids and to make sure that they complement your oral presentation. Practise not just how well your argument fits within the time limit, and how well you can communicate it orally, but also whether you can work your visual aids. It is much better to find out when practising that some part of your visual aids does not work as anticipated than to find out during the presentation itself.

7.5.3 The delivery stage

Giving the actual presentation is still a stage of the methodology, and one which you need to pay attention to just as carefully as the research and preparation stage. After all, you can research and prepare your presentation to the greatest extent possible, but if you do not make sure that the conditions are right for you during the actual delivery of the presentation itself, all of your good work could be for nothing.

Make sure that you give yourself enough time to work out how to upload your visual aids to any projection equipment and that you are comfortable with moving between slides.

Do not forget to move through your slides as you deliver your oral arguments – if you think that this may be an issue, include a prompt at the relevant point in your script or notes to remind you to move your slides on.

Index